INCEST, MURDER
AND A
MIRACLE

The True Story Behind the
Cheryl Pierson Murder-For-Hire Headlines

CHERYL AND ROBERT CUCCIO
WRITTEN WITH
MORGAN ST. JAMES

CRM Publishing

Medford, New York

www.IncestMurderAndaMiracle.com

INCEST, MURDER AND A MIRACLE

Cheryl's cry from the heart

HOUSE OF HELL

The poignant 'poem' on this page reveals the desperation that drove a schoolgirl to plot the murder of a father who subjected her to a nightmare of sexual brutality

❝ Imagine wishing you were dead, but holding on patiently by a thread that is beginning to shred more and more every minute you stay in the house at 293 Magnolia Drive — holding on because you're afraid for your sister, that might be left with a monster.

If I decided to die, how would I be able to rest in peace, knowing that my sister, that means the world to me, is going through hell because of my leaving.

Imagine hoping it was your home on fire every time a fire truck passes.

Imagine driving with your father, the man you're supposed to trust who is touching you while driving and you're hoping nobody can see you and you're praying you crash and die. ❞

Victim's story of ordeal: PAGE 7. Norman Podhoretz' comment: PAGE 20

IN 1986 NEWSPAPERS ACROSS THE COUNTRY carried stories like this one featuring sensationalized headlines like "Abused Girl Charged With Hiring Student to Kill Dad." There was even a story on the front page of the *New York Times,* and the name Cheryl Pierson was all over the media.

They couldn't get enough of it.

I met my husband Rob Cuccio when I was that abused fifteen-year-old and he has been the "rock" in my life ever since. We are finally ready to tell our side of the story—what our life was then and has been like since.

© 2016 by Cheryl Cuccio, Robert Cuccio, Morgan St. James

All rights reserved. This is a true story. No part of this book may be reproduced or transmitted in any form or by any means electronic or mechanical including photocopying, recording or by any retrieval system without permission from the authors and/or publisher except as part of a review or media article. No part of this publication may be sold or hired without written permission from the author or publisher.

Special trade paperback edition pricing for quantity purchases by book clubs. Authors are available to speak to book clubs or organizations by Skype and where possible, in person.

Email requests to admin@incestmurderandamiracle.com

ISBN-13: 978-1539660439
ISBN-10: 1539660435

Library of Congress Control No: 2016958427

Cover design: Karen Phillips
Editor: Tony Held

CRM Publishing
New York
www.IncestMurderAndaMiracle.com
info@incestmurderandamiracle.com

REVIEWS

INCEST, MURDER AND A MIRACLE is an autobiography told with extraordinary courage and integrity. I laud Cheryl Pierson Cuccio and Rob Cuccio for blazoning their traumatic pasts and valiant love story so that others who suffer in silence might be emboldened to seek help. Like so many, I was first drawn to their story for its spectacle, but have come through it deeply humbled and indebted.

~Lee Beckett, Executive Producer,
Investigation Discovery's *I, Witness*

INCEST, MURDER AND A MIRACLE is the gripping story of Cheryl and Rob Cuccio. It is the heartbreaking account of a high school student named Cheryl Pierson, who suffered years of sexual abuse by her own father. Finally, to end her torment and protect her younger sister from becoming his next victim, she arranged with one of her classmates to have her father killed. After the murder fifteen-year-old Cheryl was arrested, charged as a youthful offender and sent to prison. For some people, the horrors of that childhood would have ended any chance for a successful future, but not Cheryl. Together with her boyfriend and future husband, Rob, they overcame the obstacles, including one that appears to have been resolved with the help of Divine intervention. It's an amazing story.

~Dennis N. Griffin, author of The Battle for Las Vegas,
Surviving The Mob and CULLOTTA

A COMEBACK IN ALL ITS FORMS, from victim to survivor, from defeat to triumph, from life to death, and back again! Recovering from grief, losses, and overcoming injustice, all while rebuilding her life. This intense riveting story will have you on the edge of your seat as you turn every page. St. James helps Cheryl Pierson Cuccio and Rob Cuccio bring luminous intelligence to the impact that incest, child abuse, rape, and family violence have on a person's overall bio-psychosocial well-being.

> ~ Victoria Marion, founder and Executive Director of the Post Traumatic Stress Disorder Research Institute

INCEST, MURDER AND A MIRACLE, Cheryl and Robert Cuccio's true story that goes back to a 1986 murder-for-hire that grabbed national headlines, is written superbly in great detail with the help of Morgan St. James, who has produced fourteen published books.

> ~ GrumpyEditor.com

READING A STORY LIKE THIS makes me appreciate my childhood. I realize the problems in my early years were mild compared to what Cheryl endured. To rise up from the ashes of mental, physical and sexual abuse is amazing and I admire the strength in this woman. I can see her as a desperate sixteen year old trying to protect her sister from what she has endured and a part of me understands why she wanted her father dead. Some may wonder why she didn't just leave, but they have never experienced brain-washing through abuse, be it mental, physical or a combination. Add in the incest and the threat of having the same thing happening to her little sister, and I can understand her desperation. Thank goodness she had Rob to support her through the hard times and what turned into good times for them.

> ~Lizzie T. Leaf
> Author, Interviewer, www.lizzietleaf.com

DEDICATION

THIS BOOK IS DEDICATED TO all the abuse and incest victims and survivors out there. We can only hope that in some small way our book will help you see that you are not alone. That the horrible things that may have happened to you, and may still be happening, are not ever your fault no matter what the circumstances. We are a team and we stand together to fight this battle. We will protect each other, because we know no one else will. But we have to talk about it, tell people and bring awareness to the public. We want to thank all of the people out there who have had the strength to speak up for themself, and extend hope to other victims who couldn't speak up for themselves just yet. It is and always will be a hard journey but believe me, the journey of healing gets easier once you get the dirtiness out, rather than using all your strength to keep it in.

TO OUR DAUGHTERS—from the day you were born, you gave us the strength and courage to get out of bed every day and continue to live. Thank you for all your love, support and patience through the many nights of the read-throughs and the stress our lives and writing this book have put upon you. We appreciate all your input and always having our backs. You are both amazing human beings. You will never know or understand the pure joy or unconditional love we have for you both until you have children of your own one day.

CHERYL TO MY HUSBAND ROB— I believe with all my heart that I would not be here today if it were not for fate stepping into my life back in 1985. I know the day my mom died, she sent you (my angel) directly to find me at my locker in school. From that day on you have been, loving, protecting and taking care of me. Even in my darkest days, you never made me feel like the damaged goods I always thought I was. You have continued to love, support and believe in me through the most difficult times. This book was a grueling journey for both of us to relive, remembering all the tears, and putting ourselves right back in those scary moments. But with you by my side, we can accomplish anything. I can only pray our daughters have half a man in their lives as loving and compassionate as you. Thank you for not only being my rock, but my best friend and soulmate for eternity. I love you.

ROB TO MY WIFE CHERYL— I dedicate this book to the strongest person I have ever met. I am so lucky to have had you in my life for over thirty years. I can't even begin to think of my life without you as my soul mate. For you to have gone through everything you did and come out the other side of the tunnel as strong and beautiful as you are, is simply amazing. Thank you for never giving up on me after so many people, including my doctors, did. I would not be here to have completed this book if you hadn't been the strong survivor you are. I know that sometimes I can be difficult to say the least, but you are always there to set me straight. I am so proud of you for digging so deep into your subconscious to try to help as many people as you can. I will never forget all the tears and heartache that went into writing this book, all the rewriting and edits to get it as perfect as we could. You are truly beautiful inside and out. Thank you for allowing me to love you and loving me back the way you do. Hey, it's finally done and now you're an author—love you!

WE DEDICATE THIS BOOK TO Mom and Dad Cuccio who were always our biggest supporters and never questioned or doubted our decisions. They never once gave up on us as individuals, or as a couple. They always had the perfect advice and gave us the courage and wisdom we needed, while guiding us into thinking we made our own decisions. And, they encouraged us to write this book and always follow our dreams!

We did it Mom and Dad—here it is! We only wish you were here to see it, but you were both called to Heaven far too early. Because of your love and support it is finished- Thank you.

CHERYL—THIS WOULD NOT BE complete without dedicating this book to my mother, too. I only remember her for a short time in my life, and still try to block out most memories so I can remember only the good ones. She instilled in me the love and compassion I have in my heart. People say you learn that in your very early childhood years. Those were the years before she became sick, when we spent a lot of time together. From what I remember, life was good then. I truly believe in my heart she did the best she could and did not know about the incest. Even though I never said it as a child, "I love you, Mom. "

ACKNOWLEDGEMENTS

THROUGHOUT THE JOURNEY OF WRITING this book there were so many thanks and acknowledgements to be given out, we cannot possibly name them all.

FIRST AND FOREMOST WE WOULD like to thank Morgan St James. Not only is she an extraordinary co-author, but she is now a trusted member of the Cuccio family. Morgan, when we were put in touch with you almost a year and a half ago, we had a rough manuscript. You saw the story for what it was, and helped shape it into the book it is today. You were a bright spot for us at a very dark time. Thank you for all your knowledge and for guiding us through this process. And, for the long late nights of edits, tears and laughs. We have trusted very few with our true story, and we thank you for making this process a little easier with your compassion, understanding and expertise. We will forever be grateful for helping us bring our story to the publishing process so we can fulfill our dream of being be able to help others.

MY BROTHER JIMMY—YOU HAVE always been and will always be my Super Hero. No one could ever know how much pain we endured as children, but we got through it together then and we will continue to forever. Thank you for always being there for me and my family and never letting us down. There will never be a time I wouldn't be hopping and skipping on a moon shadow without you. I Love You- Your Favorite Sister Cheryl.

LIZ—YOU WERE OUR MAID OF honor. You never left Rob's hospital bedside and were next to us in the courtroom and the trial.

Thank you for always being there through our ups and downs. We love you.

JoAnn—Although it has been a long journey for the both of us we will always have that special bond that make us find our way back into each other's arms. Thank you for always being there for our family when we need you. We love you.

AnnMarie And James Prudenti—Thank you for all your help throughout our lives. We will never forget the first read through of our finished book. Thank you! Love you.

To all our Family and Friends who supported us throughout all of our trials and tribulations, we love you and thank you for all your support. We couldn't have gotten through this long journey without many of you. Especially Bernie Halpin for all your love and support through the years and Anthony, Deacon Bob, Birdie, Big Mike and Franklin.

A special thank you to Joanne de Simone, the local editor who was one of the first to read our manuscript. You thought enough of it to forward it to your author friend Dennis N.Griffin for consideration. We know how much harder it would have been to fulfill our dream of publishing our book without your help. Thank you.

Dennis N.Griffin— we would like to thank you for also taking your time to read our first manuscript and liking it enough to pass it along to Morgan. Your input throughout our journey has been much appreciated. Thank you.

To Tony Held, our editor—thank you for nitpicking your way through our finished manuscript. Your changes and insight were all extremely accurate. We thank you for making our book that much better.

To Paul Gianelli—your friendship and guidance has meant more to both of us throughout all these years than we can ever express in words. We appreciate that you wrote the Foreword to this book and that you take time out for us whenever we need you.

To Karen Phillips it's been our pleasure working with you on the cover of our book. Thank you for all your patience and hard work. We think it's perfect!

To Lee Beckett—thank you for making what could have been a very uncomfortable experience—our first time in front of a camera after thirty years—not be as bad as we remembered. You truly are an amazing person and one we are honored to call our friend. Thank you for all your kindness and helping us to get our story out so we can help as many people as possible.

TABLE OF CONTENTS

FOREWORD   PAUL GIANELLI 1

A MESSAGE FROM CHERYL 4

CHAPTER 1   CHERYL GOING BACK TO THE COURTHOUSE 7

CHAPTER 2   CHERYL IN MY FATHER'S CLUTCHES 16

CHAPTER 3   ROB   MEETING CHERYL...................................20

CHAPTER 4   CHERYL AFTER MY MOTHER DIED.............................24

CHAPTER 5   CHERYL MY FATHER AND ROB 30

CHAPTER 6   ROB   BACK IN CHERYL'S LIFE............................36

CHAPTER 7   CHERYL AN IDEA BECOMES REALITY.........................43

CHAPTER 8   ROB   MY PART IN THE MURDER PLOT 49

CHAPTER 9   CHERYL ARRESTED FOR MURDER 53

CHAPTER 10   CHERYL THERAPY 60

CHAPTER 11   CHERYL STORIES AND MEMORIES DURING THE HEARING ..65

CHAPTER 12   CHERYL IN JAIL 73

CHAPTER 13   CHERYL TRYING TO START MY NEW LIFE.....................79

NEWSPAPER CLIPPINGS 83

CHAPTER 14   CHERYL SETTING THE RECORD STRAIGHT.....................86

CHAPTER 15   CHERYL BITTERSWEET - MY SISTER JOANN 92

CHAPTER 16   CHERYL SIGNS OF TROUBLE 98

CHAPTER 17   CHERYL A NIGHTMARE.. 105

CHAPTER 18   ROB   THE NIGHT I DIED 111

CHAPTER 19   CHERYL BETWEEN LIFE AND DEATH.........................115

CHAPTER 20 CHERYL MY WORST FEAR CAME TRUE **119**

PHOTOGRAPHS....**124**

CHAPTER 21 CHERYL FIGHTING FOR ROB'S LIFE **127**

CHAPTER 22 CHERYL I HAD TO STAY STRONG **133**

CHAPTER 23 CHERYL MY BROTHER JIMMY **137**

CHAPTER 24 ROB   JIMMY AND I ARE CLOSER THAN BROTHERS ..**143**

CHAPTER 25 CHERYL AT STONY BROOK HOSPITAL **149**

CHAPTER 26 CHERYL CHILLED TO THE BONE WHY ROB WAS FROZEN.**155**

CHAPTER 27 CHERYL CODE BLUE...**160**

CHAPTER 28 CHERYL THE VIGIL, NIGHTMARES, AND MEMORIES **168**

CHAPTER 29 CHERYL ROB TAKES A TURN FOR THE WORSE **175**

CHAPTER 30 CHERYL DECISIONS...**178**

CHAPTER 31 ROB   BACK AMONG THE LIVING **183**

CHAPTER 32 CHERYL AFTER THE MAIN CRISIS PASSED **191**

CHAPTER 33 ROB   THE ROAD TO RECOVERY..........................**197**

CHAPTER 34 ROB   CRYING ON THE INSIDE **203**

CHAPTER 35 CHERYL LOSING MY WONDERFUL MOTHER-IN-LAW..**209**

CHAPTER 36 CHERYL MY MEETING WITH A PSYCHIC **215**

CHAPTER 37 ROB   CONSUMED BY ANGER **220**

CHAPTER 38 ROB   CHERYL AND ROB TESTIFY.........................**225**

CHAPTER 39 CHERYL NEVER SAW IT COMING.............................**232**

CHAPTER 40 CHERYL AND ROB   LIFE GOES ON...........................**239**

EPILOGUE **243**

ABOUT THE AUTHORS **247**

FOREWORD

PAUL GIANELLI
DEFENSE ATTORNEY FOR CHERYL PIERSON

THE CALL FROM MY ANSWERING SERVICE awoke me in the early morning hours of February 13, 1986. As an active criminal defense lawyer, I was often roused from a deep sleep, immediately having to concentrate on the details of a new arrest and client. The call concerned a young girl arrested for arranging the murder of her father.

A male classmate of hers killed her father and he was under arrest as well. Cheryl Pierson was in a police precinct in Yaphank, Long Island, and would be brought to court that morning for arraignment. She was white, middle class and from a community only a few miles from my home. I had become accustomed to the handling of murder cases: the clients, the stricken look on their families' faces, and the hateful stares of the victim's family and friends. I immediately sensed the case of People of the State of New York v. Cheryl Pierson was going to be very different. Cheryl Pierson was an unlikely criminal. She could've been anyone's daughter.

What could drive a typical suburban teenager to hire a fellow student to murder her father? The media and the public wanted

- 1 -

an answer. When I arrived at court that morning I saw the TV Satellite news trucks from the major New York City stations in the parking lot, ready and waiting.

I met Cheryl Pierson that morning in her holding cell and we spoke through the paint-chipped metal bars between us. She was sixteen years old—just a few years older than my daughter. Standing at little more than five feet tall and about a hundred pounds, she was hardly a threatening presence.

She wore a red and white Newfield High School cheerleader's jacket and looked groggy and disoriented. Her eyes were, blinking and bloodshot. I introduced myself and told her I needed to gather a few facts in order to prepare for a bail hearing.

This was the beginning of my long relationship with Cheryl Pierson and her boyfriend (now husband), Rob Cuccio.

It began as an attorney-client relationship. Over time I slowly became a trusted confidant, advisor, and most importantly, a friend. A lawyer never knows if a client facing criminal charges is telling them the absolute truth. From the beginning, I never believed Cheryl lied to me, but rather that she initially held back things out of fear, shame, and embarrassment. To properly represent Cheryl required exposing the fear and horror she lived with for many years. I slowly learned from Cheryl, Rob, her neighbors, and family friends the truth about her father, James Pierson. His perverted "love" of his daughter had, in effect, twisted Cheryl into a warped version of a surrogate wife.

After her mother died his demands increased and Cheryl's fear that her younger sister would become her father's next victim grew. The facts contained in this shocking book about the physical and sexual abuse suffered by Cheryl at the hands of her father, James, were recounted to me by a frightened, immature, naive sixteen-year-old girl. It was difficult to accept that her father could derive sexual pleasure from this young girl, yet it was this evidence that mitigated Cheryl's indirect involvement with her father's murder.

Reading this book, I was reminded that Cheryl is bereft of the normal, happy memories of family life many of us take for granted. I am, however, grateful and proud of Cheryl for being able to create and nourish happiness in her adult years with the Cuccio family, her husband Rob, and their two healthy daughters, Samantha and Casey.

The frightened young girl I met thirty years ago has grown up and matured. Through a determined effort she has obviously overcome the fears and shame she experienced. I am honored to have played a small part in shaping Cheryl's life after her father's murder. I am even more proud to witness what Cheryl Pierson Cuccio has become–a strong, determined woman, loving mother and wife.

Paul Gianelli, Esq.

Jamesport, N.Y.

March 2016

A Message From Cheryl

THIS BOOK IS ABOUT LOVE AND TRUST—incest, murder, and what can only be called a miracle. You see, my husband Rob and I saved each other over and over again, united a family, and my tragic story awakened the country to the taboo of being sexually, physically, and mentally abused while finding the strength to endure it all.

I was a victim of the worst kind, but finally there were a few who gave me the love and support I needed to become a survivor. For those who are fortunate enough to never have known abuse, the raw truth in this book will open the door that allows you to see into our world.

I was only sixteen years old when I hired a schoolmate to kill my father after years of sexual, physical, and mental abuse. Incest is one of those things frequently swept under the carpet, and that was especially true in 1986. No one wants to believe it exists, even now, but let's call it what it is—rape. In my case, it led to murder.

During my hearing I discovered more than twenty adults apparently suspected what was happening to me, but nobody did anything to help me! For whatever reasons they had, these adults kept quiet and never came forward until it was too late. Then there were the ones who questioned why, as the child living in such a terrorizing environment with the abuser, I had not been the one to come forward to tell anyone.

There were people who gave up on me and a lot of people who didn't believe in me, but the few that did are the only ones that counted.

I'd promised my mother as she lay in her coffin that I would watch out for my younger sister, JoAnn. That I would always protect her from my father. I was not much more than a child myself, and I was desperate. I knew I couldn't let her be raped by the monster my father had become behind our closed doors. I stood trial for arranging his murder, spent time in jail, and although helped by extensive therapy, I do have lifelong PTSD.

Throughout my hearing and afterward newscasters speculated, righteous people pointed their fingers at me, my father's relatives and so many others lambasted me. Some people said I lied about the abuse and wanted him dead for the insurance money. None of them had an understanding of what I'd endured or how successfully my father controlled me through the fear of what would happen if I didn't obey his every command. Those people couldn't feel the terror that filled me every minute of every day—the desperation that consumed me especially when he threatened to go after my eight-year-old sister. The signs were there. He had begun to do the same things to her he did with me when I was ten and the abuse had first started.

As an adult I'm not the same terrified, beaten child I was. I have risen above being a victim and found my strength. The strength I called upon when my husband needed me to be the strong one. I wouldn't give up on Rob when he was pronounced dead, and on my forty-third birthday the doctors brought him back to life after he was dead for forty-three minutes. He is alive and almost completely back to normal today—it's been called a miracle.

My desire to help other people has always been there, and I hope by writing this book it will send the message that you are strong enough to get through anything you set your mind to. If you feel you are all alone, please remember those of us who have walked in your shoes are there for you. We belong to a certain kind of club. A club no one chooses to be a part of, but once you are in you can never get out. Abuse or trauma of any kind is our bond and the reason we embrace the need to help each other.

I live by these words:

I was a victim, which can cause a lot of suffering.

There can be feelings of anger and rage that cause pain and heartache.

But you can get through it.

It can make you stronger.

It does not have to destroy your life.

It can make you fight back.

It can make you spend the rest of your life wanting to protect others.

It WILL make you a survivor always!

This book isn't just about the murder and trial. It's also about what followed. During our years of living a normal life—which was something I'd never had in my youth—we had no idea disaster would strike again.

From the day I met him, our lives have been so intertwined, my story is Rob's story and his is mine, so we wrote this book together.

As you read, you may think some of what we say is dramatized or even made up, but nothing you are about to read is fiction. Everything is backed up with documentation. Much of it is on the website www.IncestMurderandaMiracle.com

Thank you for letting me tell my true life story.

Cheryl Pierson Cuccio

CHAPTER 1

CHERYL

GOING BACK TO THE COURTHOUSE

ON THE MORNING OF JULY 13, 2015, my family and I were on our way to the courthouse in Riverhead, New York. White clouds floated in a clear blue sky. A slight breeze rustled the leaves on the trees. Twenty-seven years before, media people had flocked around the same courthouse in a frenzy trying for a "money shot" of me, a sound bite, or a headline. I was the teenager who paid to have her father murdered. I was front page news for several years.

Time had not dulled the feeling of dread that spread through me. As Rob continued along the road, visions of finding my father's bloodied body lying on our concrete driveway, the horror of the hearing, and being led off to jail in handcuffs immediately after I was sentenced flashed through my mind like images in a slide show.

I sat huddled in the passenger seat with my teeth clenched and my stomach twisted in knots, desperately trying not to yell, "Stop!" I would have given anything to never have to enter that building again.

This time I wasn't the one accused of doing something wrong.

After waiting three years, our malpractice case against cardiologist Dr. Vito Mercurio was finally about to be heard. We felt in our hearts justice would be served.

When Rob had experienced a numb left arm, chest pains, shortness of breath, and so many more signals that he was a walking time bomb ripe for a heart attack three years before, Dr. Mercurio wrote it off to anxiety and spicy food. During the six months he treated Rob, instead of ordering more tests like an angiogram and possibly admitting him to the hospital, the doctor told him, "Don't worry. Just stay away from the spicy food and cut down your smoking, and you'll be fine."

He even teased Rob and made light of his condition, saying it was all in his head.

Although Rob was concerned the symptoms he was experiencing could be very serious warning signs, he also trusted his doctor and believed what he was told. He even questioned if he was really imagining all of it. Unfortunately, his concerns turned out to be valid. The doctor had missed genuine signals that his heart was in dire trouble. Rob saw Dr. Mercurio again with complaints that the symptoms were more severe and that he'd had a frightening episode just two weeks before a massive heart attack. Once again he had been told he was okay during that visit.

I'd given my deposition two years earlier and was listed as a witness. Then, just one week before the trial, Dr. Mercurio's attorney challenged me as a witness by stating, "She was convicted of a crime and therefore not a good citizen. She shouldn't be able to testify on her husband's behalf."

That came as a real surprise. Even when I gave my deposition, Dr. Mercurio's attorney had tried to impeach my testimony by asking, "Have you ever been convicted of a felony?"

Prior to the deposition my attorney, Paul Gianelli, coached me and gave me this advice: "If anyone ever asks you if you have been convicted of a felony, say 'no.' As a youthful offender your records are sealed and nobody should ever be able to access them. You will always be allowed to answer no to that question."

But, when your life has been all over the newspapers, magazines, and television for months on end, what good are sealed records? When a book has been written by an author who only spoke to you once, but claims that the book's speculation and fabrications are your innermost feelings and thoughts, what good are sealed records? When a movie was made from the book and gave the same false impression of who you were, sealed records mean nothing.

So, in my case, sealed records were almost a joke.

It was obvious the doctor's attorney had researched my name and hoped I would say no so he could catch me lying. If he could prove I lied, I wouldn't have been able to testify on Rob's behalf. An internet search for Cheryl Pierson still turns up pages and pages of information about my life—some true, some pure fantasy or the invention of a writer's or reporter's concept of me.

Maybe he waited until a week before the trial to challenge me again as a strategy to get me thrown out as a witness. When he entered his objection, Dr. Mercurio's attorney had only referenced the felony part. He didn't mention he was referring to the nearly thirty-year-old sealed case of a youthful offender, or that I'd been a good citizen ever since. I paid my debt to society, but have never been truly free of the control over my life.

As Rob drove along the road to the courthouse in Riverhead I thought about the latest ploy by the defense to keep me from testifying. The week before the trial I had to force myself to drive there alone to get proof that the records were sealed and I'd been a youthful offender.

As we got closer to the courthouse, it took everything in me not to turn back—not to run away so I wouldn't have to face my past. But, of course, I couldn't do that. Visions of the trial all those years before swirled in my mind like demons, teasing and tormenting me. My breath came in short bursts. My heart pounded like a crazy drum solo, accompanied by the ringing in my ears. I knew the signs and had tried to fight off what always came next when PTSD kicked in with a major panic attack. I couldn't let that happen. I had to get the documents. I needed to be able to testify. I had to be there for Rob.

Bombarded with visions of how I'd struggled to keep our family's dirty secret for so many years until it suddenly became front page news—the case on everyone's lips—I fought the rising panic with everything in me. In my mind I was once again a scared sixteen-year-old badgered by reporters who demanded I answer their questions.

"Did you love your father, Cheryl?" one would shout.

"How long was the sex going on?" another would ask.

Throughout the trial my father's sister and mother sat in the spectator section giving me what I called the stink eye. Cheryl Pierson—the main attraction in a show of the damned.

In a matter of minutes, all the years of trying to smash everything down so tight it could never penetrate my waking consciousness was gone. I couldn't even hear the music playing on the radio. All I heard in my mind were echoes of the past. Reporters and crowds shouting at me.

"Cheryl, over here! Look this way, Cheryl."

I imagined the harsh glare of the neon lights in Room 100 in Suffolk Criminal Court—a long windowless room. The sound of the incessant whir of the ceiling fans that had cooled the room pounded in my head while the sound of every footstep crashed and echoed off the bare floors.

By the time I pulled into a parking space, my face burned like it was on fire while my body was chilled. When I adjusted the rearview mirror to check my makeup before going into the building, wild eyes filled with fear stared back at me from a red-tinged face.

INCEST, MURDER AND A MIRACLE

Breathe deep. It's okay! You can do this—you're safe. That was a long time ago. Get out of the car. You need to do this.

I opened the door with shaking hands and a hammering heart, then walked into the building that held only nightmares for me.

Once inside the Criminal Records Department, bile rose in my throat. Barely glancing up, the woman behind the desk handed me a slip and said, "Here, fill this in with your name and the date of the case."

When I handed it back, she looked at it and said, "Uh, this case was almost thirty years ago."

I said, "I hope you have..."

She cut me off in mid-sentence. Her eyes narrowed to slits. Her voice dripped icicles. "I *know* who you are," she said sharply as she locked eyes with me. I guess people have long memories.

I managed a tentative half-smile. "Okay, then can you get the file?"

Twenty minutes passed while I waited, hoping no one had heard our conversation.

I'd lived my life with honesty and integrity—tried to be a good role model to my girls and lived up to the person my dead mother would have been proud of. And now I'd been reduced to standing there telling a stranger I was a criminal.

The woman finally came back. "Sorry, I couldn't find your file anywhere."

What? Droplets of cold sweat beaded on my forehead. I needed her to find that file. I had to be able to support my husband's case.

"Is that because the case is so old?"

"No. I found your co-defendant's file and his case was the same date as yours." She held out a piece of paper with a court stamp on it. "This says you were a youthful offender. That's all you'll really need. If I do find the file, I'll get back to you."

- 11 -

I never heard from her.

Back in the safety of my car, I shut the door and stared at the paper clutched in my hand. First my body shook violently, then the tears came—slowly at first, then building until I sat there sobbing uncontrollably. *Is this really all there is of my horrible childhood? This one piece of paper?*

I had to pull myself together as I've done so many times before so I could drive back to work to finish my day.

❖ ❖ ❖

I looked over at Rob, confident at the wheel and filled with so much anticipation. He was breathing heavily, clearly in deep thought. This was going to be our time to shine. It was our family against them and we would win this battle! We were right and the doctor was wrong. Or so we thought.

I aimed the rearview mirror toward my girls sitting in the backseat, then pictured myself as I'd sat in the backseat of Birdie and Big Mike Kosser's car, on the way to my trial in 1986. They were the neighbors who had taken me under their wing, and although everything had been very stressful for them too, they never gave up on me. I loved them dearly. My girls were a lot older now than I was at that time, Sam twenty-three and Casey twenty, but they still looked like babies to me. I could tell how nervous they were, just like I was—and I still am.

In an effort to calm myself, I looked out the car window taking in the trees and grass, such a rich shade of green. Somewhere birds were chirping, filling the air with their sound. When we walked into the courthouse all polished up, we looked like the perfect family. Rob cleanly shaven with his hair slicked back, wearing black dress slacks and a nice button-down dress shirt, me in a black skirt, starched white blouse, and black high-heeled dress shoes. Sam and Casey, so professional looking in stylish pants topped by conservative blouses.

We had been alerted there might be reporters hoping to cover our story and were worried about how our daughters would react. To our relief no reporters were to be seen.

When you first walk into a courthouse, you have to pass through a metal detector just like the ones at an airport. Although that never really bothered me in an airport, this was different. We were across the street from the jail where I'd served my time and I was close to freaking out.

I inched up to the metal detector and froze. Although I tried to keep walking, I couldn't move. Instead I began to shake. *Don't touch me, please don't touch me.*

The only way I was able to force myself through the detector was to keep repeating in my mind, *That was then. This is now. You aren't in jail and won't be patted down by a guard. You can do this.*

When I was in jail, every day after my visit from Rob and my brother Jimmy the officer in charge made me strip down and patted down my body everywhere that something might be hidden. I remembered praying to God to make it stop. *God, my father terrorized me for years. He raped me, he hit me. How can you let this strange man make me undress? He's touching my private parts. Please make it stop!*

But it went on day after day and I've never been able to get past that feeling.

The only reason I managed to get through those terrifying pat downs without complaining out loud was that it meant I could enjoy seeing Rob and my brother Jimmy, who came together to visit me every day I was in Riverhead County Jail.

As we approached the courtroom, I steeled myself to enter a courtroom very similar to the one in my nightmares. Our attorney and Rob's sister Liz were waiting for us. At last we would be able to confront the doctor who almost cost Rob his life. I'd never actually seen him, and until now we just called him names like Dr. Death because as we found out in the worst way possible, he should have taken the combination of Rob's symptoms as the warning of something very serious.

Dr. Vito Mercurio appeared to be about our age, kind of short and stocky, dark hair, and he had a mustache. His suit was nice. He wore a tie. The man walked with his head down and shoulders up in a hunched manner.

At first I wanted to race up to him and shout in his face "How could you?"

During the three long years we waited for our day in court, I'd dreamed over and over about how I would react when I finally saw him. To my surprise, I just faced him and stared directly into his eyes. It was something I never had the courage to do to my father —confront the person who hurt and changed my family forever. I made him look at me while I fixed him with a cold stare.

No longer the victim, I gave him no choice but to look at me and see what was reflected in my eyes. I hoped somewhere deep down he would feel the impact of what he'd done.

In the past I'd been the one who woke up screaming almost every night, tormented by a nightmare. Now, thanks to Dr. Mercurio, Rob woke up almost every night, too, haunted by nightmares about coming out of his coma and not being able to breathe or scream for help.

In my nightmares, I always have a pillow over my face so I don't have to see my father or have his awful smelling nicotine breath in my face. He lies on top of me pushing his three hundred pound body back and forth and ramming into me—his sick way of satisfying himself. The sight of Rob and me screaming throughout the night could almost be material for a black comedy routine if it wasn't so terrifying.

Before the hearing began, the judge said, "This letter about Cheryl Cuccio's youthful offender status is enough proof for me to allow her to testify on Robert Cuccio's behalf."

The doctor's attorney protested immediately. "But, it doesn't have her name on it."

The judge answered, "The case number is enough information. There is no name because of the sealed record status."

At least the judge agreed to let me testify, but would my past ever stop playing a role in my life? Would it always dictate how I must live?

I hadn't been in a courtroom since my trial for my father's murder. This felt like a repeat of the accusations that had been hurled at me so many years before. Dr. Mercurio's attorney was determined to make me look like a dishonest person who would lie on the stand. Resentment coursed through me, but I knew I had to control myself. Gradually I settled down and felt my tense muscles begin to relax.

If I'd thought going to the Criminal Records Department the week before was bad, having to sit there in the exact same courthouse where I'd been tried and convicted was far worse. Over the years I'd managed to make it seem as though all of it happened to someone else. Now it took every bit of my self-control not to run from the room screaming. By focusing on my beautiful family sitting next to me, I managed to stay as calm as possible. I told myself this man we were facing would pay for what he had done. He had almost stolen the family we created and worked so hard for when he failed to recognize that Rob was a strong candidate for a fatal heart attack.

Deep inside I was proud I was not the defendant this time.

CHAPTER 2

CHERYL

IN MY FATHER'S CLUTCHES

I'D NEVER NOTICED ROB UNTIL I met him in gym class at Newfield High when I was fifteen years old. At the time, I really liked a boy named Glenn, although I wasn't allowed to have boyfriends or date. People thought it was because my father was strict. I never dared tell them the truth. How could I let anyone know his being strict was the least of my problems? James Pierson was viewed as a successful man with a bit of bad temper by everyone who knew him. Nobody would have believed he was also a very possessive, jealous, sick person who wanted my feelings and love only for himself and used his teenage daughter for his sexual pleasure whenever he felt the urge.

I had to work hard for my grades, but was a decent student and kind of quiet. School was very important to me. It was the only place I could be myself. When I was there I could try to forget about my mother being deathly ill, about taking over the role of mother to my younger sister, and all the wifely chores I had to do, including the worst of them—the constant sex with my father.

I was popular in school, and it was the only place I felt I was like everyone else—just a kid with lots of friends.

My father was a big man. Some would describe him as burly. With his bushy red eyebrows and freckled face, his hair short and brushed to one side, some people even thought he looked boyish. When he was young he was an athlete and had hoped to pitch for the Yankees someday. That never happened. Now, out of shape, he carried a large belly. His hands, like his six-foot frame, were massive and rough. But it was his mind that was so warped.

When he wanted to scare me, he'd say, "Don't think you're not being watched when you're at school. You know your principal is my good friend and he lets me know everything you do. So, you'd better watch your step. If you do something wrong, I'll know before you get home, and you know what that means."

You bet. It probably meant I'd get a beating. I knew they had gone to school together and were still friends. As an adult, I am not sure the principal really did report back to him, but it was definitely strange that some days my father knew exactly what I had done at school. He was able to tell me all about my day, as though someone was monitoring my every move. He always finished by saying, "Good thing you didn't do anything wrong or I'd know about it."

He never let me go anywhere after school, but if my mother wasn't in the hospital she would sometimes allow me to go to my best friend MaryAnn's house. MaryAnn covered for me and let my parents think I was with her at her house. Instead, we rode our bikes to Glenn's house or sometimes the three of us would meet somewhere. As long as my mother thought it was just MaryAnn and me hanging out it was okay. In his arrogance, I'm sure my father never thought I would want to show love or affection to any male besides him, so I was terrified he'd find out I had a secret boyfriend.

Flashbacks are common with PTSD, and sitting there in the courtroom, I found myself reliving the day I first met Rob in gym

- 17 -

class. I remembered I was a little sick to my stomach and not in the best of moods. Rob had walked over to me with a swagger and a funny look on his face.

"Hey, you" he said, acting like he was one of the guys on the *Sopranos*, "you're dancing with me." Then, he turned and walked away.

One thing my father always taught me was not to take any shit from anybody. I know that seems ironic since I took so much from him, but he always said, "Don't ever start the fight, but if it happens, always make sure you finish it. If you don't, you *will* pay the consequences when you get home."

I wasn't a bully by any stretch of the imagination, but I also wasn't afraid of anyone other than my father, and didn't take any shit from anyone else. What could possibly be worse than what was already happening to me? Think about it. My mother, whom I loved dearly, was dying. My father, whom I hated, was raping me on a regular basis besides beating me. I tried to get good grades in school, was a surrogate mom to my sister and responsible for cooking the meals and cleaning the house. Did I have time to be a normal teen? Hardly. My father made sure my little bit of free time was spent in his bed.

So I kind of had this chip on my shoulder. When Rob acted so arrogant, I just thought he was a jackass. Well, we did dance, and one of the moves was the bunny hop. I wasn't sure what his game was, but he positioned himself behind me, and when I jumped back he purposely jumped forward at the same time causing my butt and his crotch to bang into each other. *What the hell was this moron doing?*

When the dance was over, he picked me up, threw me over his shoulder, and spun me around, and that made me feel even sicker. I ran into the bathroom and threw my guts up. So yeah, the first time I met Rob was not very pleasant for me.

As time went on, I didn't give him much time or attention, but he kept trying. One day I saw him walking down the hall holding some other girl's hand. I guess that was a wakeup call because from that time on I began to be really nice to him. Until we became good friends I had no idea he had asked to be transferred into my gym class. Then he told me, "I switched because I saw you around and wanted to get to know you better."

How different my life might have been if Rob had never switched to my class. Once we were together, everything about him seemed cool to me. He had a car and drove to school. I thought that was cool. I hated when my parents smoked, but when he smoked that seemed cool to me, too. In fact, as I sat there in the courtroom thinking about it, I realized I'd looked at everything he did that way for years.

The only one in our house with a horrible truck driver mouth was my father, and I hated every nasty word he used. Other than that, no one cursed, not even my mother. Rob cursed while talking or telling a story—I thought that was cool, too. Right from the start he was always able to make me smile, no matter how bad things were for me at home. Nothing he did ever seemed to bother me.

After all these years of being together, people ask us "What's your secret?" and both of us always say, "I married my best friend. You need to be friends first and be able to have fun and always have trust in that person."

❖ ❖ ❖

I was aware of the low hum of voices around me in the court-room, but tuned them out. Lost in memories of sitting in the same courthouse so many years ago, accused of taking my father's life, I glanced over at Rob sitting beside me, alive and mostly recovered from the heart attack that almost took him from me permanently, and gave a little prayer of thanks.

CHAPTER 3

ROB

MEETING CHERYL

I MET CHERYL AT NEWFIELD HIGH SCHOOL in 1985 after I'd dropped one class and decided to take another gym class. I was a senior, she was a sophomore and a damn good looking one at that. The moment I saw her walk in, I knew I had to make her my girlfriend. I wasn't sure who she was, and didn't know anything about her, but I was determined to find out.

I kept asking around to see if anyone could tell me anything about her. Finally a goofball I knew named Craig, also a sophomore who happened to be in the same gym class, said they were friends.

I am a big believer in Fate.

This kid Craig was always getting into trouble with the seniors, so I'd helped him with his problems and even got into a few fights for him. When word got around that Craig was my boy, his problems stopped, so he was happy to introduce me to Cheryl.

Fortunately it was the time of the school year when we had to square dance in gym. All the guys in the class knew who I was gonna ask to dance, so none of them even tried to get her to dance with them. You see, I was a big guy in school and liked to fight.

- 20 -

Everyone knew I wouldn't hesitate to throw down, especially over a girl. When it came time to ask for a partner, I went over to her and said "You're dancing with me."

She wasn't too interested in me, or so I thought. I know what an asshole I must have sounded like, but something must have worked because she finally said, "Okay."

Things took off for us after dancing. By Valentine's Day I was going to ask Cheryl to go steady with me and bought her one of the red carnations the school was selling. I looked for her, but couldn't find her. I'd finally gotten up the nerve, and this was a great opportunity to give her the flower and ask her, but I couldn't find her anywhere. I was totally bummed out.

There I was, walking around the school holding this stupid flower with nobody to give it to. On my way to my next class, I turned a corner and there she was at her locker. Fate I tell ya— kicks in every time. I still had the flower and I was all ready to give it to her, then ask her out. I tapped her on the shoulder with a big smile on my face. When she turned around, she was crying, and I had no idea why. I dropped my outstretched arm holding the flower and said, "Hey, please don't cry. I'll throw it away."

"It's not the flower, Rob. M-my mother died. She had this rare disease and fought it for years, but it's over now. She died." Tears streamed down her face and all I wanted to do was hug her. Anything to make her feel better.

Cheryl took the flower and said, "We're having a wake for her. Will you come?" She gave me the information, grabbed her books, and ran out.

The next day I went to her mother Cathleen's wake and met the rest of Cheryl's family. It was a very somber experience. The thing I think about these days is what if I never went down that hallway and saw her that day? What if she never told me about the wake?

Would I still be alive today?

Anyway, our relationship took off after that, but we became good friends first. Cheryl's father was very strict and she wasn't allowed to date anyone. I had to be her friend first so I could get to know her father. In the beginning he and I actually got along pretty well. I think he respected me for going to the wake and making his daughter happy.

We talked a lot, me and her dad, but the more I got to know him, I had this strong feeling something wasn't quite right in his relationship with Cheryl.

I knew he was pretty well off—not rich, but well off—and nothing was too good for his daughter. When she turned sixteen, her party at the Island Squire Restaurant was one of the first Sweet Sixteen parties I had been to. It was like a wedding. We danced and partied, and I was even able to drink alcohol.

When it was over I was kinda drunk and had to drive Craig and myself home. Another one of my friends was at the party and we started to race on this two lane highway. I was in the wrong lane when out of nowhere a car came around the bend headed right at us. To this day I don't know how we didn't die that day. I like to think Cheryl's mother or maybe even my guardian angel were looking out for me because they knew I had to stay alive to protect Cheryl. Whatever force kept us safe, we missed crashing by millimeters and milliseconds.

On June 6, 1985 I finally asked Cheryl to go steady. From that time on, her father always made sure he got in the way of our happiness. I couldn't figure out why his attitude toward me changed. Even though I broke up with her multiple times, something or someone always made me go back. It wasn't just that she was hot—it was this inner feeling that she needed me and I knew I couldn't leave her.

I couldn't explain the bond that grew between us, but I had never fallen for anyone like I did for her. I knew one thing for sure—something definitely wasn't right at her house. The more I was there, the more I knew the relationship with her father wasn't normal.

CHAPTER 4

CHERYL

AFTER MY MOTHER DIED

EVERYONE ATTENDING THE FUNERAL TRIED to comfort us kids and hugged us to the point where I sometimes felt smothered. Whenever I tried to have a minute alone with my mom's body, some well-meaning person intruded. At last we had a minute alone—just me and my mother. I sat beside her body, so still and cold in the coffin, desperately feeling the need to tell her how sorry I was for never really saying I loved her. I was terrified she would be watching over us from Heaven now, seeing everything we did—even watching me having sex with my father. I had to explain that I never wanted it to happen.

I looked around to make sure no one was near us and lowered my voice, just to be sure. "I hate the way he touches and uses me, Mom, but I can't stop him, no matter what I try. I promise I'll protect JoAnn." My voice cracked and tears streamed down my face. "Please don't hate me for what you see Daddy doing. I promise I'll do whatever it takes to protect her and I'll take care of Jimmy, too."

Just for a moment the room seemed to grow warmer. Maybe it was my imagination, but I told myself she heard me.

Then I had to tell her I had someone to protect me, too, so I added, "Mom, I have a friend who will protect me. Rob is a great guy and really seems to care about me. He's lent me his strength ever since you went into the coma, and I only wish you'd gotten to meet him. Please don't worry. Rob will protect me. I know it."

I sat there by myself a little longer, thinking, *Did you know you were going to die? Maybe you sent Rob to me—the one person I would be able to trust. Maybe you knew he would be the one I'd finally be able to tell what was happening to me.*

Right before someone came in, I said out loud, "Mom, ask God this for me: 'Why did he decide to take the wrong parent? Why you and not him?'"

Just after I said it, I realized the answer. God doesn't want bad, evil people in heaven. He took our mom because she was an awesome person and he wanted her with him. Still, the doubt lingered in my mind. Maybe I was wrong and he felt I didn't deserve to have her.

I'm really afraid of him, God. Things would have been so much better if my father was the one you took, but now she's gone and I'm stuck with him. I'm so alone.

Looking at it as an adult, I wondered if my mother might have suspected my father was molesting me but was too weak to do anything about it. Still, I would like to believe that she didn't know, and to this day I'm thankful she didn't live to see what I was finally driven to do.

Even as she faded away more each day, I'm sure she knew what a hard time I would have after she was gone. Now I hoped she also knew Rob would protect me and take care of me because she couldn't. Wasn't that how things were supposed to be in a perfect world? Some days I could actually convince myself that fantasy was true. Other days I just felt so angry that God took her from us.

After the burial everybody went back to their normal lives,

the house was pretty quiet, but my father's sexual abuse became more frequent and harder for me to handle. I was overwhelmed with guilt, believing in my heart my mother was watching from Heaven. I became obsessed with hoping she had heard what I'd said as I sat by her coffin. *Do you know how much I hate what he makes me do, Mom? I loved you so much!*

◆ ◆ ◆

With Rob in the picture, my father had found something new to hold over my head.

Whenever he demanded sex, he'd say, "You have to do this if you want lover boy to be able to come over," and I would obediently do whatever he commanded. He had a tendency to explode easily, and could make it very miserable for you if you didn't do what he wanted. By then I was so beaten down, some days I gave into him simply to keep the peace.

If I didn't cooperate, he'd sulk like a child and most times the sulking turned into hitting or punching. It was much easier to do what he wanted than to try to fight him off. With my pillow pressed over my face while I tried to hold my breath until it was over, I got pretty good at making my mind take me to a place where he didn't exist as he slammed into me.

I thought about things like my plans for the next day in school, or an event I looked forward to. On the really bad days I just prayed to my mother to forgive me and kept telling myself how much I hated what he was doing. Every time I felt his heavy breathing on me, I'd wish for it to stop for good. I tried very hard to imagine this wasn't happening to me but to someone else. I always hoped the ordeal would be over faster that day. And, yes, sometimes I did wish he would die!

When it was more than once a day, it took longer each time. I got tight and sore and that's when he would say, "Pretend I'm Rob. Try to enjoy it!" That made me even more sick to my stomach. I'm sure that's a big reason I wasn't able to enjoy sex with Rob for a very long time.

Once my father was satisfied, the rest of the day was usually bearable unless it was one of the days he wanted more. Sometimes as much as three times a day.

Rob saw how overwhelmed I was and helped in every way he could. He even mowed our lawn when he came over. After years of physical abuse and ridicule by my father, my brother Jimmy had moved out. He wasn't allowed to come to the house, nor did he want to, so in addition to every other responsibility, my father made me mow the lawn, too.

Rob finally said, "Listen, Cheryl, you've got all you can do to handle everything your father makes you do. I'll mow the lawn from now on and whatever else I can do to make it easier for you," and he took over whatever manly chores I was made to do. It amazed me that although Rob thought my father was a dick, and my father was jealous of him, they actually got along pretty well. That is, until he began to view Rob as a threat to his secret sexual abuse.

My father had a recording device on our home phone that he kept in the basement. I found that out the hard way when Rob called me one day and asked what I had been doing.

I said, "I'm eating an ice cream cone."

He asked, "So, are you licking it?"

I laughed at that. "Yes, I'm licking it."

Then he said in a playful way, "I wish I was that ice cream cone."

I just laughed.

Later when my father came home, he immediately went downstairs like he did every day. I'd always thought that was an odd thing to do, but that day I discovered the reason for his daily trips to the basement.

He stumped up the stairs like an animal and glared at me,

anger flushing his face and eyes blazing. When I asked, "What's the matter?", he said in a nasty way, "So you like to lick ice cream, huh?"

The feeling of my heart sinking when I realized he was taping all of my calls is something I can still feel to this day. Right after he asked that question, he beat me until I cowered in a corner hoping to ward off his blows. From that day on, Rob and I never had a private conversation over the phone.

I'd like to think I received whatever good qualities my father had except for his bad temper. Growing up I was pretty quiet, like my mom, and I never liked confrontation. I always tried to be the "peacemaker" because I didn't want anyone to be mad or upset, especially at me. My father had conditioned my obedience well by using abuse and degradation. Maybe that's why I never told anyone what was going on and meekly submitted to his quirks and demands.

In a small way I'm still like that, but now with everything I've gone through with Rob being sick, then dying, I speak up. Life made me tough. When you go through what I did, you have some choices. Remain the meek, battered person or get stronger. I got stronger and will never allow myself to be a victim again. You have to stand up for your rights. If I hadn't, Rob would not be with us today.

That's part of the reason I decided to write this book. I may sound like I'm preaching, but always ask yourself questions and, if in your heart you don't feel something is right or fair, speak up. Because of my father's violent temper, I never had the opportunity to do that as a kid. As a result, I still trust only a small number of people and I don't think that will ever change.

Telling this story makes me very sad, but it will help you understand what a cold, heartless person my father was and that I wasn't the person often portrayed in the media.

When we were growing up, we had a blonde poodle named

Cocoa. The only reason we were allowed to have a dog was that my mother wanted one. I knew Cocoa would never hurt me, and showered her with love. When my mother became too sick to do anything, I did everything I could to avoid my father.

He never bothered with Cocoa until my mom wasn't able to care for her. One day I came home late from visiting my Mom in the hospital and remembered Cocoa hadn't been let out all day. Poor Cocoa had peed on the floor. When my father saw that, he kicked her so hard she bounced off the wall, then cried for hours. He wouldn't let me go near her to comfort her. She kept crying and it made me so sad I wanted to die. She was never the same again, and not long afterward, she died. I never forgave him.

I was just a kid, but as I look back I often question why I hadn't had the courage to defy him that one time and comfort her anyway. I loved her so much. When she died, I prayed to her all the time and hoped she heard me

Can you hear me, Cocoa? I'm so sorry. I should have held you.

After my mom died, I felt some peace about Cocoa's death. My mother would take care of her in Heaven and it would be okay.

CHAPTER 5

CHERYL

MY FATHER AND ROB

RULES IN OUR HOUSE WERE RIGID. When Rob came over for dinner it was very stressful, but I secretly enjoyed it. My father made us eat a certain way. No drinking was allowed until everyone was finished eating. There was no talking at the table, either. You had to eat counterclockwise at all times. First a scoop of meat, then potatoes, then vegetable, in that order. If you broke the cycle and didn't continue to eat that way until everything was gone, there were consequences. We kids weren't allowed to eat just one thing in whatever order we wanted, nor could we even eat one thing at a time. I used a lot of ketchup to wash down the foods that were so dry. In fact, people still laugh at me because of the amount of ketchup I use. Old habits die hard.

I hadn't prepared Rob for those crazy rules. So there he was—the dinner guest who didn't know how things were supposed to be done in our house. He practically drove my father over the edge by eating whatever he wanted, in the order he wanted, while my father squirmed in his seat itching to say something nasty. Watching that scenario play out was one of my great pleasures. I loved seeing my father struggle not to shout at

Rob.

When Rob drank during the meal and talked instead of being silent, my father clenched his teeth, but never said a word. I sat there, overjoyed at his discomfort. Of course, I was too afraid to ever ask, but I always wondered why he never made Rob abide by his rules. Maybe deep in his twisted brain there was a realization that his rules were so preposterous he was actually embarrassed to tell Rob that he had to eat according to "The Rules of James Pierson."

My father knew he wouldn't be able to keep an eye on us if I was out from under his iron fist, so I was never allowed to go to Rob's house. If Rob wanted to see me, he had to come to our house, and my father always lurked nearby.

Desperate thoughts ran through my mind all the time.

What if I could go out with my friends like other kids? But, Jo-Ann—I can't leave her alone at home with him. Gotta protect her. Promised Mom.

Once I was actually allowed to go to see fireworks, but when I came back the house was dark. My heart pounded as I ran inside, terrified for my little sister. *JoAnn? Is she okay? Why did I go?*

The only light came from the television in my father's room. I rushed down the hall to his room, and sure enough, my sister was lying right next to him with her little head on his bare chest, sound asleep.

I didn't have to say anything. The look on my face said it all.

"Go ahead," he mocked with a leer stretching from ear to ear. "Keep going out with your *boyfriend*, and you can be sure I'll spend more time with your sister." The lecherous expression on his face left no mistake about what he meant.

When I questioned my sister the next day, she said, "Daddy and I were just watching TV, and then I fell asleep." I didn't think anything had happened. Most likely he gave me that leering look to threaten me.

- 31 -

The summer after my mom died, Rob and I had some troubles in our relationship. By then my father was getting on his nerves. He was tired of never being able to go out like normal teenagers. Whenever he came over, he just sat on the couch with JoAnn and my father to watch TV.

Finally, he broke up with me and my heart was crushed. We were supposed to be boyfriend and girlfriend but I didn't want him to touch me or let him get close to me. That was something he couldn't understand. Like most teenage boys, he'd wanted me to do what he wanted me to do, but I couldn't. How could I tell him it wasn't him but what my father was doing to me?

When I found out he was dating other girls—going out and having fun with them at Great Adventure and other places like teenagers should, I was sad and angry at the same time. During that time I hated my father even more. He had ruined everything in my life and on top of it now he was happy Rob wasn't coming around anymore.

He'd say with a triumphant note in his voice, "Ya see, he didn't love you. He only wanted to get into your pants."

I was depressed all the time and lost a lot of weight. I couldn't eat or sleep. My thoughts weren't filled with Rob during that time. It was much worse than that. The thought that my mother could see what was going on between her husband and daughter haunted me day and night. I'd rationalize that maybe she was happy the guy I loved was probably with other people. Maybe she wanted me to know the pain she felt while watching me and my father having sex.

Were these rational thoughts? Of course not, but I was living in torment every minute of every day. The only time I ever felt safe was when I was able to escape to a secret place in my mind where I could live out any fantasy I invented. A good life. A perfect life.

I was convinced the two people most important to me hated

me now because they both left me. Some days all I could think of was wanting to die. The thing that might have saved me from becoming a teenage suicide statistic was the promise I'd made by my mother's casket. *I won't leave my little sister with this monster.*

❖ ❖ ❖

That September I was happy to get back to school. I got all new clothes and finally started to feel good about myself again. My days were filled with more than cleaning the house, cooking, having sex with my father, taking care of my sister, and wondering who Rob was with that day. At last I felt I was over him when to my surprise he drove up to see me while I was at school.

He was now in his first year of college and I never in a million years expected to see him at Newfield High again. When he walked up to me, I ignored him. I was so angry he'd chosen to come back into my life right when I was finally getting over him.

We went back and forth, and I finally gave in. He came over that night and it was as though we'd never been apart. Except for the time I spent in jail after my father was murdered, we have never been apart since.

"Look," I told him, "I understand where you were coming from. My life sucks and yours doesn't have to. I can't blame you for wanting to have fun, but nothing's changed. My father is as bad as ever, maybe even worse, and I know if we were together we couldn't have much of a relationship. He watches me like a hawk."

But Rob wasn't having any of that. He said, "I missed you, Cheryl. I'll stick around until you're older. Maybe then you'll have some freedom. I want us to be able to do fun things together and act like normal people. Lord knows, you deserve it."

The more time Rob spent at my house, the more he seemed to be asking me a lot of questions about the relationship between my father and me. It got harder and harder to keep things hidden from him. When Rob was at our house, my father did everything to show him that I was *his* girl. However, by showing his possessiveness, I don't think he realized that he was also giving away his secret.

◆ ◆ ◆

That Christmas Rob's parents invited our family over for Christmas Eve dinner. I was shocked my father agreed, but we did go. He still acted as though he liked Rob and said he wanted to get to know his family.

I was really nervous, worried my father might do something to embarrass me. I was happy to be able to spend time with Rob for the holiday, but tense and on guard the whole time. His parents seemed to like my father, though. I think they felt sorry for him having to raise his children on his own. They actually respected that he was so strict with me. Maybe they thought because he was strict I was a good girl and wouldn't give them any trouble.

How shocked they would have been if they even had a hint of what our family life was really like. How would they have reacted if they knew this strict man, a man they appeared to like, was having an incestuous relationship with his own daughter, their son's girlfriend? Would they have welcomed me into their home if they had any idea of what was to come?

But that Christmas Eve they liked me and my family.

Rob's Christmas present to me was an ankle bracelet with our names on it. Ankle bracelets were very popular back then, and if you had one it showed everyone you were taken. The bigger, the better, and mine was really big. It had lots of diamonds and was so special to me. It was the first piece of jewelry I had received from a boy, and I loved it.

My father, not so much! He had to let me wear it that night

and I was allowed to wear it while I was around Rob, but I was absolutely forbidden to wear it any other time. He hated that bracelet, and took it away from me as a punishment any chance he had. In his mind I was his, not Rob's.

I was embarrassed about the gift I had for Rob. Next to the ankle bracelet it seemed insignificant. Although my father wouldn't let me buy a gift for him, I saved up for two months or more so I could buy him something. I went shopping at the mall with a friend, and I bought a Christmas stocking ornament with his name engraved on it. We still have the ornament that I was so embarrassed to give him, and place it on the front of our tree every year. I also bought him some of his favorite candy and a few other small inexpensive items. I think he was surprised because he knew I didn't have a job like he did, and he certainly knew my father would never allow me to buy him anything.

Rob and his family made that first Christmas without my mom the best they could for us. I will always be grateful for their kindness.

CHAPTER 6

ROB

BACK IN CHERYL'S LIFE

THE SUMMER OF 1985 WAS A VERY DIFFICULT one for me. There I was in love with a girl named Cheryl, but every night I had to leave her house by eight or eight-thirty. My own curfew had been increased to two in the morning and I had nothing to do after I left. Many nights I hooked up with one of my friends and we hung out until I had to go home.

One night I was with my friend Mike and his girlfriend Bari. We went back to her house where I met Sue, Bari's friend from New Jersey who was visiting for the summer. Well, I was a young guy and when I saw Sue I decided if I couldn't be with Cheryl after eight o'clock, why not spend time with her. My hormones were raging, she was pretty good-looking and willing to fool around. I figured I could keep it from Cheryl so she'd never have to know. At this point you're probably thinking again, "What a dick."

Unfortunately for me, one night Sue put a few hickies on my neck. After I went home and saw them, I knew I wouldn't be able to see Cheryl until the marks went away. My house was between Cheryl's house and the school, and wouldn't you know it? The next morning while I was outside, Cheryl stopped by unexpectedly while riding her bicycle home from her Driver's Ed class. Any other day, that would have been great, but this day I had those damn hickies on my neck. It wasn't going to be good. She looked at me with such disgust and disappointment, then said, "This is what you do after you leave my house? Screw you Rob! I never want to see you again," and rode off. I stood in my driveway not sure if I was relieved she broke up with me or what.

At least when I was with Sue she restored my confidence. I kept thinking the reason Cheryl would never fool around with me was my fault. At that stage I definitely had suspicions but didn't know for sure that the strange relationship between Cheryl and her father included incest.

Then the summer was over, Sue was back in New Jersey, and I really couldn't stop thinking about the mistake I made with Cheryl. All I knew was I needed her and deep inside I knew she needed me—I had to try to get her back. I made myself wait until school started because I didn't want to just show up at her house.

As I drove to the high school, I rehearsed what I was going to say if I could find her. Well, maybe fate had something to do with it, but Cheryl was outside on lunch break. She saw my car and kinda went the other way. I didn't even park in a spot. I jumped out of the car and yelled, "Cheryl, Cheryl come here, I really need to speak to ya."

She stopped and looked at me, and I wasn't sure if she'd let me say what I had to say. I couldn't tell if she was angry or just didn't care.

"Look, I need you to know that I never stopped thinking about you the whole time we've been apart. I'll never do something as stupid as that ever again. Just let me come over tonight and talk to you."

She finally agreed to let me come over that night. After I groveled for a while, she gave in and took me back, but said, "If you ever do that to me again, I'll leave you and never return."

- 37 -

You know, that rule still applies to us today—I have never been unfaithful to Cheryl since that summer in 1985. I can do virtually anything else wrong and she will forgive me. However, I know there is no way she would forgive me for cheating on her again.

◆ ◆ ◆

Life went on as usual and the seasons changed. It was December and I was going to buy Cheryl this ankle bracelet for Christmas. We had spoken about it, so she knew I was going to get it for her and she was bubbling over with excitement. The problem was I had wanted her to be surprised when I gave it to her and realized if she knew she was getting it she wouldn't be surprised.

This first Christmas without her mom would be hard on her and I really wanted to make it as special as I could. I bought and paid for the ankle bracelet in early December and kept it in my dresser drawer for almost a month.

Cheryl's father actually allowed her to go to the movies with me one night, and in my rush to get there I got a speeding ticket. I had no idea her father followed us to the same movie and later found out he even sat behind us watching our every move. That's how possessive he was. Imagine my surprise when he said, "I saw you getting that speeding ticket, Rob. I won't allow my daughter in your car if you can't obey the speed limit." And I thought he had finally allowed Cheryl some freedom, but instead he spied on us.

"Sorry," I said. "I know I was doing fifty-five in a thirty mile zone." Well, he didn't want to hear my excuses, but he did forgive me and allowed us to continue the relationship. However, after that he got even more possessive and I was beginning to get extremely uncomfortable about the whole situation.

Then I hit upon an idea of how I could surprise her with my gift. I said, "Cheryl, I'm so sorry I won't be able to get you the ankle bracelet we talked about. After I pay the speeding ticket, I just won't have enough money left, and my mom said I can't pay for both."

Of course, that was a lie, because the bracelet was already in my dresser. I knew she was upset and I was sorry about that, but so happy she believed me. I'd be able to surprise her on Christmas after all.

The next time I was in the Pierson home, Mr. Pierson grabbed me and took me into his garage. His voice was gruff, tinged with anger, and he tightened his grip on my arm. "How come you're not getting Cheryl the bracelet?" Before I had time to recover from the surprise that he even knew about it, he took out a wad of cash and tried to shove it in my hand. "If it's a money problem, I'll help you out. How much do you need?"

"That's okay, Mr. Pierson. I already got the bracelet and I just wanted her to be surprised. I figured that wouldn't happen if she knew she was getting it."

"She told me you couldn't get it for her because of the damn speeding ticket you got going to the movies. Not only that, but she said your mother wouldn't let you pay for both. Since you already got the bracelet, how much is the ticket? I can pay for that."

His eyes had a funny gleam, and there was something about the way he insisted I accept his money that I didn't trust. "That's okay. I'll just put in more time on my job at the supermarket so I can pay for the ticket. Thanks for offering, though."

Even then he didn't give up and persisted in pushing the money at me. I'd already seen his nasty temper on a different occasion, and I didn't want to set off him off. For a minute I thought it might be much easier to take his cash, but then I stayed firm and said "no" again.

He shook his head and hissed at me, "Okay, but don't bring your mother into your lie. Cheryl just lost her mother and it wasn't a good idea to do that."

After thinking about it, I knew he was right, but now the lie was out there and I couldn't take it back. I said, "I'm sorry, you're right. I'll never use my mom in a lie again."

Looking back and knowing everything about his sick mind that I do now, I'm sure that in some crazy controlling way he was determined to help pay for the ankle bracelet so he could tell Cheryl it was partially from him. I am so glad to this day that I never took his money. I also think he might have respected me for not taking the easy way out even though he was really pissed off.

When Christmas came, she was so surprised and happy, and it made me feel great after I'd caused her so much pain that past summer by being a dick. She bought the nicest ornament for the tree and some candy she knew I liked. It was the greatest present I ever got from a girl. I really liked the fact she did the best she could with the little money she had. She still has her bracelet today and I still have the ornament. Somehow I don't like her buying me anything, though. The fact that she puts up with me and my shit is present enough.

◆ ◆ ◆

The more time I spent at Cheryl's house, the more I knew things weren't right, but I'd told myself I wouldn't push her. It was no secret she had all she could do to live with her father's demands and crazy rules.

Finally, one day we were fighting and it just slipped out. Without thinking before I spoke, I said, "I know your dad is sleeping with you. I know it. Don't ask me how, I just know it."

Cheryl's eyes widened as she looked at me in shock. Color rose in her cheeks, then her eyes flashed with fear. "No, Rob. You're wrong. He...I...um, he isn't. What gave you that idea?"

"I know I'm not wrong—I see it. I see the way he touches you and hovers over you. The way he looks at you and I see the jealousy in his eyes if I touch you. You can tell me. Please. We have to talk about it."

She broke down then, touching off a waterfall of tears. "I didn't know you could see it. He forces me, and now I'm afraid he's going to go after JoAnn. He's been doing it to me a long time. Please, please don't repeat this to anyone. I'm so afraid of him. And, my sister is only eight years old. I have to protect her."

I was stunned. Until then I'd only suspected it, but now she had confirmed my worst fears. *WOW, now what?*

That conversation changed my life forever. As soon as the words left her mouth, I knew I could never leave her. I feared for her and knew how much she needed me. Looking back, I often tell myself if not for that conversation and my life as it unfolded, I wouldn't be here to help tell our story. If she hadn't fought for my life like a tiger when I couldn't, I would be dead.

Even with no money and no job prospects, I was ready to run away with her—just pack our bags and go. What did I know? I didn't think it would be the best life, but anything would be better than what she was living.

Then I looked at her standing there ashamed, tears rolling down her face, and my anger against Pierson soared. *That poor girl!*

Like I said, I was a fighter, and at that moment I didn't care how big he was. I couldn't even imagine what it would be like to have the one person you trust the most—the one who is supposed to protect you and raise you—beat you and rape you over and over again.

She deserved so much happiness after enduring what she did for so long, but what was I going to do? How could I help her? Suspecting it was one thing, knowing was another. There I was, a seventeen-year-old boy who finally knew why the girl he loved couldn't stand to be touched, with nowhere to turn for advice or help. I certainly couldn't ask my dad, because I'd be betraying her. He was a former cop and would insist upon filing the right

- 41 -

complaints with the police. On the other hand, I couldn't leave her in this situation so I could find a different girlfriend and live happily ever after. I just couldn't do that.

No matter what solution I thought of, it wasn't going to work.

Fate stepped in again with a news story about a woman who contracted someone to kill her abusive husband.

There was a hesitation in Cheryl's voice when she said, "You know the story in the news about Beverly Wallace, that abused woman who paid to have her husband killed?"

"Yeah, I saw it."

"Well, maybe it's my way out. I've been talking to this guy in homeroom and he said he thought he would be able to kill someone. We...um, we're talking about hatching a plan."

The thought was so bizarre, all I could do was laugh. "Don't hold your breath. It will never happen. People say a lot of things, you know, until it's time to actually do something."

I was still trying to figure out how to get her out of the hellhole of a life she was in, never thinking the kid would actually kill her father. I even went so far as to meet with Cheryl and Sean, the boy from homeroom. I drove them to her house so he could scope out the area. She was so desperate by that time, I only did it because I thought it was what I should do for her sanity. Like I told her, it wasn't going to happen.

Weeks after the fateful day when I drove them to the house I received the phone call that would change my life forever again.

CHAPTER 7

CHERYL

AN IDEA BECOMES REALITY

WE HAD DINNER EVERY NIGHT BY SIX O'CLOCK so my father could watch his favorite program, the Six O'Clock News. As usual, we kids were sitting at the table eating our food counterclockwise in rotation—meat, potatoes, vegetables—never daring to break the cycle. We were not allowed to watch the television during dinner, so we just listened.

Once in a while if something sounded interesting, I forgot about not being allowed to watch, and for a quick second turned my head and got caught up in whatever grabbed my interest on the TV. When that happened, if my father realized I had broken yet another of his crazy rules, he would give me a hard slap across the top of my head. That always stunned me into remembering I wasn't supposed to be watching TV.

On that particular night the commentator was talking about a woman named Beverly Wallace from around our area who hired someone to kill her abusive husband. I sat there chewing my food, trying to appear uninterested.

What a great idea if you knew the right person to do the killing.

- 43 -

It was one of those idle thoughts that sometimes pop into your head when you hear something. I don't deny often thinking about what it would be like if my father wasn't around, but lots of people think thoughts like that. It doesn't mean they would do anything about it.

In the 1988 book about my case, the *New York Times* reporter wrote: "Cheryl never read the newspaper and almost never listened to the news. She was one of those teenagers whose world was not affected by current events."

That couldn't have been less true and showed how little she really knew about me. I listened to the news every night when my father did and of course I was interested in what was happening in our town and in the world. She made it sound like the only things that interested me were shows like *Divorce Court* and *General Hospital*. To add insult to injury, by putting in print that I didn't even know the name of the Vice President or New York governors' names, she made me sound like a totally clueless airhead. You can't imagine how angry that made me. She wrote it and readers believed I was who she said I was.

After hearing about the Beverly Wallace case, the details of what she did troubled me all night long. I thought about that husband beating and abusing her. *My father could be gone forever, just like that.* That thought repeated over and over again in my mind as I tried to sleep. Being only sixteen, I imagined the killing part would be like something on a TV show. I wasn't thinking in terms of bloody reality, only that he would be gone forever—I would never have to suffer him touching me, raping me, or beating me ever again, and I'd have kept my promise to my mother. My sister would be safe.

The next day, after my sister was asleep and he'd summoned me to his bed, I was still thinking about it as he began to touch me and start his usual ritual.

Please, God. Let it be over. Don't let him ever do this again. I prayed for salvation, as I often did, knowing what was coming next.

I kept hoping one day he would realize what he was doing was wrong and just stop. Instead, as time went by the sex increased instead of decreasing.

At one point I became so stressed, I stopped eating because my stomach was always in knots and I didn't care if I ever ate again. I lost a ton of weight. In fact, I lost enough that teachers questioned whether I was sick. I wanted to say something, but fear ruled. I kept quiet, afraid that if I did say anything and my father found out, it would get worse than it was. After all, the teacher would have to tell my father's friend, the principal, and by the time I got home, he would know. I could only imagine what he would do to me.

I kept losing weight, until one day when I stood up my pants slid practically to my knees even though my belt was cinched to the smallest size.

That could hardly go unnoticed, and my English teacher called me over. "Cheryl, are you okay? You've lost so much weight, I'm worried."

I just smiled and said, "I'm fine, but thanks."

That night when my father pulled me on top of him by my arms, he pushed my shoulders back and forth with his tight grip, until I couldn't move my arms. I tried to move out of his grip, but couldn't. My mind screamed, *Don't hold me like that, please don't do this to me,* but my voice remained silent.

I was pinned in such a way that I couldn't cover my face with the pillow like I did when he was on top or behind me. I stared straight ahead at the portrait of Jesus over his bed so I wouldn't have to look at his crazed, flushed face.

He yelled, "Your fucking tits are shrinking down to nothing." Then he slapped them and shouted, "Look, you have nothing left. What the hell are you doing? No guy wants a flat-chested bitch."

I laid there and took what he dished out, but my thoughts were running rampant. *I know what to do. If I don't eat and keep losing weight he won't want me. He'll despise me and won't rape me anymore if my chest is small.*

But unfortunately that wasn't the case. The more I lost, the more he complained. He couldn't force me to eat when I wasn't around him, so losing weight and pissing him off because my breasts were too small for him seemed like a good thing to me. It was the one thing I could have control over.

On the fateful morning after hearing about what Beverly Wallace did, I went to my desk in homeroom. We were seated in alphabetical order, so I sat right behind Sean Pica.

The TV broadcast I'd listened to about the murder played in my mind, I looked at him with only one thought. *Maybe he would know someone I could hire to get rid of my father.* I'd never really talked much to him before. I was part of the popular crowd, and he wasn't. It was also rumored that he hung out with a bad crowd. Because everything was so out of control when it came to my father, I never tried cigarettes or did drugs. I had a fear of not being in charge of myself. I am a control freak now and I like things my way. Maybe that's because I had no control over my life when I was younger and never want that feeling again.

I tapped him on the shoulder and said, "Hey, Sean, did you hear about that lady Beverly Wallace who hired someone to kill her husband?

He turned to me and answered, "No, what's that about?"

"Well, when I was listening to the TV last night, ..." Then I told him the story and wasn't nervous as I talked about it. At that point I had no idea our conversation would turn into my asking him if he would kill someone.

Until things calmed down after the teacher called our names for attendance and we recited the Pledge of Allegiance, it was kind of noisy in our homeroom. Nobody had been listening to what we were talking about.

I'm not sure where it came from, but all of a sudden I heard myself say, "Wow, who would be crazy enough to be hired to kill someone?"

There was silence for a moment. Then Sean looked me in the eye and said "I would if the money was right."

Whoa! Sean would commit murder?

There I was, a sixteen-year-old girl who had been horribly abused for five years, and I feared the same was about to happen to my eight-year-old sister. Like I've said, teenagers don't think like adults, and at that moment I sure wasn't thinking about legal consequences or even what it meant to take a life. All I could think of was being free. Without considering what could happen if someone actually killed my father, with no concept of the awful reality of such an act, I questioned, "How much would you ask to do it?"

"A thousand dollars!"

My mind raced like a train pulling away from the station and my heart pounded so hard it felt like it would jump out of my chest. *A thousand dollars? That's it?*

It was as though Heaven had just opened up to me! I couldn't believe it. Was a thousand dollars my answer to having this monster never be able to touch me again? Never be able to transfer his sick assaults to JoAnn? My father always kept money in the house and it was an amount I thought I could get my hands on. It wasn't a fantasy anymore.

I leaned closer to Sean and whispered, "If you're serious, I know someone who would like to hire you for that."

He whispered back, "Who?"

After taking a deep breath, still feeling like this was unreal, I breathed, "Me!"

Our teacher had stepped out, but now was back in the room.

While everyone paid attention to the teacher, I was lost in a cloud of joy. It felt like I was tap dancing on air—like I had just won the lottery. I couldn't believe it.

"I'll be in touch about it," I said in a barely audible whisper.

I didn't think about what it would mean for my father to be brutally murdered—the only thing in my mind right then was the abuse would finally stop and my sister would never have to deal with it. Who wouldn't end their misery for a thousand dollars!

CHAPTER 8

ROB

MY PART IN THE MURDER PLOT

OUR PHONE RANG EARLY IN THE MORNING on February 6, 1986. My mother picked it up and called up the stairs, "Cheryl is on the phone."

I picked up the phone in my room and immediately knew something was up. She should have been in school.

Without saying anything to soften the blow, she blurted out, "My father is dead."

"DEAD?"

I could barely make out what she was saying through her sobs. "Yeah, something happened to him in the driveway."

"Okay, calm down. I'll come over. Don't worry."

She said, "No, the police are here now. I-I've got to go. I'll call you later." And she hung up.

I can still picture how I jumped up with my fist in the air and put a hole in my ceiling. When she heard the noise, my mother came up to my room from the kitchen. "Rob, what happened?" she asked in a concerned tone.

"Cheryl's father died."

Her concern turned to shock. "Oh, Rob, I feel so bad for

Cheryl. She has no parents left now."

After she left my room, I sat on the edge of my bed thinking about what my mother just said, and began to cry. I knew he didn't just die. I knew he had been murdered. I wasn't sure if I was crying for her or for me, but now I was involved in something really big and didn't know what to do to get us out of it.

Cheryl called me later that day after the body and the police were gone, and confirmed what I already knew. Sean had actually killed James Pierson.

"How did it happen?" I asked in a strained voice.

Cheryl choked out, "He shot him—five times. In our driveway."

"I'll be right over," I said and drove to her house.

When I got there, her Aunt Marilyn, her father's sister, was at the house going through every nook and cranny looking for Cheryl's father's safe. The thing that struck me was that she didn't seem very upset her brother was dead, and it was also obvious Marilyn didn't know where the safe was.

Cheryl said, "Keep watch and let me know when Marilyn's coming. I'm going to the safe but I don't want her to see where it is. My father always has money in it, and now that Sean has really killed him, he'll expect to be paid $1,000."

This was bizarre, like something out of a two bit movie. Cheryl couldn't figure out how to open the safe, so she gave me the paper with the combination on it and asked me to open it for her. I knew what she was doing was wrong, but I still worked the combination until I heard the click. Then I said, "Just go in there and turn the handle and it should open."

When she did, the safe opened, so I never felt I was lying at the hearing when the District Attorney asked if I opened the safe and I replied, "*No*, I didn't open the safe, Mr. Jablonski."

Almost thirty years later, the answer would still be no.

That District Attorney tried his hardest to lock us up forever, and literally freaked out when I told him I didn't open the safe. You see, I may have worked the combination, but as far as I was concerned the handle had to be turned to complete opening it. I figured I only did one part, but never actually turned the handle or pulled the door open.

When Cheryl opened the safe she counted the money and there was only four hundred dollars. Sean would demand his thousand dollars and I'd only have four hundred for him. I knew it wouldn't be good, but it was what it was.

A few days later I met with Sean and delivered the money. Somehow deep down neither Cheryl nor I really believed he would do it, but now the deed was done and I was really nervous. I handed him the money and said, "Look, chill out. We'll pay you the rest when we get it."

Sean didn't fight like I'd thought he might. He took the money, agreed, and we went our separate ways.

Cheryl and I went through the wake and funeral and tried to act like we knew nothing. It's one of the hardest things I've ever had to do and something I will never forget. When you've died and come back like I did in 2012, there are definitely things you forget, but we'll talk about that later. The one thing I know, even dying didn't alter that awful memory.

As I left Cheryl's house a few days later, a car behind me flashed its headlights. I pulled over to see who it was and the next thing I knew, I was in an undercover police car going to headquarters. I was scared and didn't know what would happen next.

When we arrived at headquarters in Yaphank, the officer took me upstairs, and showed me they had Cheryl's brother, Jimmy. The cop said, "Robert, we know everything."

Being young, dumb, and not watching *Law and Order* on TV every hour, I didn't ask for a lawyer and answered the questions they asked to me. The next thing I knew I was under arrest. Then they asked me to go with them to arrest Cheryl because it would be easier for her if I were there.

I did it for Cheryl so she would know it was going to be okay—that we would do this together the right way. I remember how they pulled into her driveway with me in the backseat of the police car. I wasn't handcuffed, but was still in the back of a police car trying to figure out what I was gonna say to her. I had to look her in the eye and tell her we were in big, big trouble. It is another feeling I will never forget.

The only comforting thought was now she would be able to sleep at night and didn't have to wonder if her father was going to creep in her room and rape her yet again. At that moment I was willing to lay down my life for her, and that has never changed.

The next year was very rough for us both individually and as a couple. It seemed everyone didn't want us to be together and they were doing everything in their power to keep us apart.

One thing nobody really understood when they tried to break us up or keep us apart was that it was only making what the two of us had stronger. Looking back, I guess I have to thank them. There had to have been a force keeping us together back then. Despite all the fights we had, all the people trying their hardest to keep us apart, and finally the law and the courts succeeding in doing just that, nobody or nothing could come between us. The force was so strong then and is just as strong even now.

When I had a massive heart attack on her forty-third birthday and had no pulse, no oxygen to my brain and didn't breathe on my own for almost an hour, even that couldn't break us apart. I'm alive and here to tell my part of the story only because of Cheryl, my soul mate, who had become a very strong person due to everything she went through in her life. Today she is a woman who stands up for herself and refuses to be a victim ever again. For that I am the luckiest man alive.

CHAPTER 9

CHERYL

ARRESTED FOR MURDER

THURSDAY, FEBRUARY 13, 1986, EXACTLY one year to the day after my mother died, was also the day we were arrested. I was asleep when the detectives came to my house sometime after 12:30 that night. My aunt came into my bedroom, woke me up, and said, "There are some detectives here who want to speak to you. Get dressed and come into the living room."

I did what she said, and saw Rob standing next to my grandmother. There is no denying that I was scared.

The detective said in a flat but commanding voice, "Cheryl, do you have something to tell your grandmother?"

I answered, "No" in a low voice, but then Rob said, "It's okay, Cheryl. They know everything."

What he said took a minute to sink in, and then I began to cry. I felt like I was in a nightmare. *Could this be happening? Will everyone know my filthy secret now?*

One of the detectives looked right at my grandmother and said, "Your son was killed because your granddaughter paid someone to do it."

Upon hearing that, she began to wail.

The detectives took me away in their police car, and in my confusion I didn't know if I was relieved or mad at Rob for telling them what happened. The ride to the police station was very quiet. Neither Rob nor I said anything, and neither did the detectives.

Once we got there, they separated me from Rob and I was all alone. The detectives asked me questions for hours as I sat there shivering in this cold room while admitting details of the sex my father forced me to have with him, between my sobs. I had never talked about some of those things before. Not even Rob knew the complete details, and now I had to tell these two men, these two strangers, details of my life and the secret I had carried for six years.

Rob, Sean, and I were led into Courtroom 100 in Suffolk Criminal Court for arraignment— a windowless room with fake wood paneling on the walls. Neon fixtures bathed everything in a harsh, unnatural light. Ceiling fans buzzed as the blades moved stagnant air around, which only increased the feeling that the walls were closing in on me. I tried to take a deep breath, but it was more like a gasp. My heart felt like it had skipped beats. The horror of what happened was real and I couldn't escape it.

I still wore the same Newfield High jacket I'd worn the day before when we were arrested. That jacket was always so special to me—one of the few things that made me feel okay and normal. Being a cheerleader and representing my high school football and basketball teams was an honor I didn't take lightly, so I felt a little funny wearing it in front of a judge who was about to charge me with a crime.

My aunt Marilyn sat at one side of the courtroom with my grandmother and a family friend. Sean's father, a stocky former New York City policeman, sat at the other side. Rob's father, Robert Cuccio Sr., also a former New York City police officer, later a detective, sat with his wife in another part of the room. The three groups had no connection to each other except the murder, but they all wore the same expression: disbelief.

My attorney, Paul Gianelli, entered the courtroom from the rear door and walked down the middle aisle. Mr. Gianelli was one of the best-known attorneys in Suffolk County, and luckily, thanks to the recommendation of a family friend, my aunt had hired him to defend me. A friend of the Pica family who knew him also implored him to represent Sean, but he had already been retained as my attorney.

When we were finally called, Rob was first. He pled not guilty to a charge of conspiracy, and his bail was set at $5,000. His father paid it on the spot. Then it was my turn. I stood there handcuffed, wearing my school jacket and sweatpants with tears pouring down my face. Mr. Gianelli told the judge, "She has been a virtual prisoner in her home for the last five years. Her father was six foot two, and she is five foot two. She did all the work around the house. Students have seen her with black and blue marks from the brutal beatings she suffered. There was intercourse forced on her by her father, and one of her concerns was that he was ready to do the same to her eight-year-old sister."

My bail was set at $50,000. Mr. Gianelli insisted they had to find a way to get me out of jail. I was pregnant.

Two of my father's friends signed a cash note for $25,000 each which was accepted, and I was released on bail ten days after my arrest.

That was the beginning of the media circus. The reason my case attracted so much national attention was because of the disturbing moral and social issues it raised, and its potential for legal precedent.

If the case went to trial, it was believed, a jury would have been asked to consider whether incest is grounds for justifiable homicide for the first time, testing whether the kind of sympathy that courts have granted to battered wives and others subjected to sustained violence should be extended to abused children as well.

Although I'd never gotten along very well with my Aunt Marilyn, she was appointed as my guardian and I had to live with her while I was out on bail. She did everything to make it obvious to me that no one close to my father believed the stories of sexual abuse—not even the men who posted my bail. Later, after I miscarried, DNA testing proved the fetus was Rob's. All those people who never believed me about my father's incest felt that proved I was lying about it.

◆ ◆ ◆

During the time I was out on bail, I tried to adjust to having freedom and acted like a normal teenager as much as I could. Most people didn't understand it was the first time in my life I was ever able to do that. I worried constantly that this could be the only time I'd be able to enjoy this kind of freedom for a very long time. I pled guilty to manslaughter and was obsessed that if things didn't go well during my pre-sentencing hearing, I could be locked up in a jail cell for many years.

The date for my hearing finally came on the morning of September 9, one of those beautiful Indian Summer days when the rich green of the trees contrasted against a brilliant azure blue sky.

If you think having sex with your father is scary, you should try being on the stand waiting for the judge to hand down your sentence for his murder. The courtroom was packed with relatives, people who knew the families, curiosity seekers, reporters, and sketch artists. It wasn't a big courtroom, just three long wooden rows, but excitement and anticipation radiated through the rather small space as though an electric current had taken over.

Reporters followed me into the courthouse every day,

INCEST, MURDER AND A MIRACLE

screaming questions while they banged into me trying to get their cameras and recorders directly in my face. I was terrified when these strangers constantly screamed shameful questions at me. There was no escape. Their attitude was no different than if they were asking what kind of ice cream I liked. My dirty secret was out to the world, and these reporters yelled their questions about incest and murder at me with no compassion or consideration of the embarrassment or fear they were causing.

To make matters worse, I had to face my grandmother, Virginia Pierson, and my aunt Marilyn every day of the hearing. They may have been my aunt and grandmother, but I knew they wanted me to go to jail for a long, long time. This might sound strange, but I actually understood why. If someone killed my child or one of my siblings, I would really be pissed off, too. I don't think I'd be able to control myself. So, although I could understand the stink eye they were giving me, I was still a scared teenager very intimidated by their presence.

In my heart I felt they knew what my father was really like. Sometimes I thought that he turned out like he did because of all the stuff my grandmother put him through as a child. My grandmother would probably never have admitted to doing it, but she should have known that she screwed him up, and that he was indeed capable of sexually molesting his daughter. I won't go into what I believed she did to my father when he was growing up, because I'm not sure how much of it is true. Many of the stories I was told certainly made me believe my father endured some level of abuse for him to turn out the way he did.

Despite knowing that so many of the people in the courtroom were sure I was lying, and that horrible false stories about me were circulating, I did have a lot of support, too. Rob and his whole family were so awesome to me. By living with our neighbors, Birdie and Big Mike Kosser, after I left my Aunt Marilyn's house, and being able to spend time with the Cuccio family, I experienced what a real family was all about for the first time in my life. I saw how you are supposed to protect and love and trust each other without inflicting hurt. I loved all of them more than I can ever say.

My brother Jimmy paid a lot of money to Paul Gianelli for my defense, and Mr. Gianelli was wonderful to me. We became quite close after we had a few heart-to-heart talks. As restricted as my life was, I was pretty mature for my age, and the more he knew the real me, the more he realized it was my life and I could make decisions for myself.

I am honored that Mr. Gianelli has written the Foreword to this book. I guess he saw something good in me, because we've remained friends all of these years.

Throughout the time I was out on bail and afterwards when I was in jail, Jimmy and I became close again. Not having lived in our house since my mother died, he finally learned how messed up my life really was. I needed and depended upon him and, as the saying goes, he stepped up to the plate for me. Rob and Jimmy became very close during the hearing and later while I was in jail. I was so grateful they never deserted me and always had the reassurance they were ready to protect me at all costs.

At that point, I was just starting to trust my therapist, and I'd made a few friends, like Deacon Bob. I met him after coming out of jail on bail during the brief time I lived with my aunt, before I moved to the Kosser's house.

My aunt lived next to Saint Margaret's Church and I used to walk there and sit inside to get away from her. I'd never liked her to begin with, but it got worse after they placed me in her care. She made it so obvious that the way she saw it, I'd had her brother killed. Her anger toward me was so strong that resentment constantly hung heavy in the air. Not a great combination. I went from being physically, mentally, and sexually abused by my father into a very bad, tension-filled situation with my aunt. The only good part was that I was still with JoAnn, but as the tension continued to rise, I finally reached the point where I couldn't take it much longer.

I used to walk to the church where Deacon Bob spent time talking to me. It turned out Deacon Bob had umpired Little League games during the time my father coached Jimmy's team. He said he often had to throw my father out of a game for cursing and screaming at the young players. So many people kept insisting my father had been a good guy, and here was Deacon Bob remembering him as a complete asshole around the children. Small world I guess, but I don't think I could have gotten through the time I was at my aunt's house without him.

When I visited him at the church, he always made time for me. We had many conversations about what had happened and the challenges I was facing. He talked about how God always forgives and everyone eventually gets to Heaven.

I think Deacon Bob told me that so I wouldn't feel like I was a bad person, but he didn't know I was actually asking him questions relative to my father.

Sometimes when things really got tough for me, I considered just ending my life instead of going to jail. I knew my sister was somewhat safe, I craved peace, and desperately needed my mother. I don't think Deacon Bob ever realized he probably saved my life when he told me everyone goes to Heaven and God forgives all. The idea that my father could be in Heaven and if I died I would go there too, made me decide to stay right where I was.

On earth I'd be as far away from my father as I could get. If there was the slightest chance he was in Heaven, I wasn't going there before my time. Having finally gotten away from him, I wanted to keep it that way no matter where I ended up.

CHAPTER 10

CHERYL

THERAPY

AFTER I WAS ARRESTED, I SPENT A lot of my time at the therapist's office. In the beginning I really hated those sessions and gave the doctor a very hard time. I had worked so hard to push all the horrible memories down to the depths of my soul where I wouldn't have to acknowledge them or think about any of it ever again. I simply couldn't understand the logic of bringing everything up again.

I used to tell my therapist, "It's not like talking about everything that happened will change anything. It happened and it's over, so why do I have to talk about it? Why make me relive it over and over?" Secretly I felt that because she never went through the nightmares I experienced, she couldn't hope to understand any of it. I couldn't accept that I needed to release the poison I was harboring.

For the first time in my life I was just trying to take care of myself, and boy was that different. I was so confused, that it tore me to pieces emotionally. Sometimes it felt like the walls of that office were crushing me, and there was no escape. Sometimes I refused to even try to talk about the worst things. At other times, all I could do was cry. What purpose did it serve? That's what I kept asking myself.

In fact, I really got pissed off when the doctor continued to push me to talk about things I didn't want to face. The more she continued to make so much of what I'd managed to push down rise to the surface, the more it became the reality I needed to acknowledge. I often thought, *This is disgusting. I'm so embarrassed.* Sometimes I even said that out loud.

The thing was, I'd never told anybody all the details, not even Rob. And now I sat there with tears streaming down my face telling a stranger.

But, it worked, and after several sessions I did begin to feel a little better about myself. It was as though a big burden had been lifted from my shoulders. I still cried torrents of tears, but my thoughts began to change. The emotions I'd shut off just to survive were coming back. *So this is what it means to feel like a human being.*

Through talking it out in therapy, I learned my father was just a very mentally sick man who needed help and may not even have been the totally evil man I thought he was. More important was the realization that it was not my fault. I had done nothing wrong to cause him to do the things he did to me. I wasn't the dirty pervert who brought on the shocking incest as many had insinuated or actually believed.

Make no mistake. I still hated him, and I will resent him for stealing my childhood until the day I die, but I did learn to deal with the pain. Some people say they forgive but not forget. Well, it's the opposite for me. I try to forget, but cannot completely forgive.

We talked about a lot of other relationships I was dealing with—my brother and sister, and Birdie and her family. When the therapy began, I had just left my Aunt Marilyn's house and moved into the Kosser's house. With the sessions releasing hideous memories and dumping me onto an emotional rollercoaster, it was a stressful time for everyone.

Birdie's daughter, AnnMarie, went from always being the only girl in the house besides her mother to not only sharing her bedroom with me but also her bed.

Every night I feared the nightmares that were sure to begin as soon as I drifted off, so sleep didn't come easy. Then, after I finally did fall asleep, if AnnMarie's body accidently touched mine I'd wake up immediately in a panic, not remembering that my father was dead. Cold sweat slicked my body. For the moment I'd be back in the past and knew what was sure to come next. Then when I looked at AnnMarie, I realized the danger was gone.

As hard as everyone tried, it never really felt like I belonged there. I desperately needed to have some privacy, something I didn't even know the meaning of, but it was clear that wasn't going to happen. They were all so concerned about me when all I wanted to do was shut myself away.

Before I went to jail there was the stress of not knowing how things would turn out, and I obsessed over it. How long of a sentence would I receive? What would happen to me? All I wanted was to be able to be happy and do what I thought were normal things for the first time in my life.

The Kossers did their best and tried to emphasize to me how important it was to keep a low profile. Paul Gianelli wanted me to lay low and stay indoors. That just added more stress for everyone.

I said, "Look, I have no idea how much freedom I'll ever have. What if I'm sentenced to the fifteen or twenty years they are asking for? What if I get life in prison?"

They tried to explain how important appearances were to the public, but I was convinced no one saw it the way I did. How could they? They weren't the ones who were going to be locked up.

"Give me a break already," I'd shout. "I just want to do things any other normal teenager would do, like maybe go to the movies or hang out and watch television at Rob's house. I feel like I'm a prisoner already. Don't you understand? I only want to enjoy something in my life before I go to jail."

I couldn't understand the harm in these simple things. Maybe part of what I was experiencing was teenage bitchiness, but I'd been on a short leash for so many years. If only I could feel like everyone else, even if it was just for a short time.

Stories in the media and all the notoriety made it impossible for me to go back to school, so I continued to get home schooling in order to earn my high school diploma. I also worked full-time at a hair salon as a shampoo girl. I went to BOCES Career and Technical School to finish my schooling as a cosmetologist and really loved it there. Along with all of that, I had to fit in therapy sessions twice a week.

As far as I knew, no one at the beauty school knew about me or if they did, no one let on that they knew what I'd done. While I was waiting for the hearing, I finished the course and received a temporary license. Unfortunately it expired by the time I needed to take the state test because by then I was in jail.

I'd received my driver's license at the age of sixteen, so I was able to drive back and forth to work and to my therapist's office, and that was the only time I ever had to myself. While I drove I did a lot of thinking—some good and some not very good.

Several of Sean's friends were very angry and felt I'd ruined his life when I asked him to help me. More than once they tried to run me off the road while I was driving, so it was important for me to always be on the alert. In all honesty, I did partially agree with them. However, that didn't make it any easier or less scary when they followed me, hell bent on forcing me off the road. Maybe even trying to kill me.

There were so many issues my therapist and I had to talk

about. One of the most important things on the agenda was for her to try to prepare me for the jail term, as much as possible anyway. We had to talk out in the open about how I would be able to deal with that.

When you've experienced what a hell is like, it gives you strength for what might come. At that point I felt anything was better than my father's constant abuse and sick incestuous desires, so I was ready for the challenge.

I knew the hardest part would be being away from Rob. He was my support team, always protecting me and making me feel better about myself. In jail I'd be on my own.

CHAPTER 11

CHERYL

STORIES AND MEMORIES DURING THE HEARING

I WAS JUST SEVENTEEN AND ROB WAS nineteen when the day of the hearing finally arrived. From the time we met I always knew Rob was in my corner. We had to grow up very fast after my father's murder and both of us were scared. We had no idea where our lives would end up or how we would deal with whatever happened.

Rob was given five years probation, but when it came to me, public opinion was split. Some reporters insisted I had to pay for what had been done, and painted me in a very bad light. Others rallied to my support and were against jail time for me. Much of the public prayed for me not to go to jail and I felt they understood what I'd lived with and what finally made me break. I sat in the courtroom day after day, listening to the testimony of all of the witnesses. It was even hard to hear some of what the ones on my side said—often things about my family I'd never heard. Worst of all, I had to relive every moment that led to my father's murder every single day.

They told stories about my parents and spoke about events that occurred while I was a small child. I learned some of them thought my father hit my mother in the back, causing kidney damage, and that's why she suffered so many kidney problems. She had two kidney transplants while she was sick and apparently she also had a rare blood disease that attacked her kidneys. Beginning when I was about ten she wasn't home with us kids most of the time during the six years she was sick. She underwent four hours of dialysis three times a week while she waited for the kidney transplant. In the end, it wasn't the kidney disease or blood disorder that killed her.

The ceiling fans kept filling my ears with that whirring noise, while I listened to what the various witnesses said while I fought back tears. I fought so hard not to break down.

Toward the end, my mom got pneumonia. I don't really remember if we were given a reason why she couldn't fight it, but suspect she must have been too weak by then. All of her organs shut down and put her into a coma before she passed away. When some witnesses talked about my father hitting her, that broke my heart. I never saw my father hit her, but clearly pictured how she was so afraid of his temper. To this day I don't know why she put up with the way he talked to her or the way he treated her, but the more I heard, the more I realized she must have been deathly afraid of him.

Then there were the witnesses who spoke on my father's behalf. They said things like, "He was a great, kind man who would give anyone who needed help the shirt off his back."

I didn't dare laugh out loud at testimony like that, or even give a slight smile, but I did laugh inside my head at how he'd fooled them all. Mr. Gianelli had cautioned me not to show my true emotions because if I even cracked a smile, the news reporters would have a field day on the front page of the newspaper the next day.

Yes, I thought, *my father was an asshole.* My brother Jimmy and I were his punching bags, but I never actually saw him hit my mother or my sister. Thinking about how he terrified us brought back the memory of the day he drove me to school on Valentine's Day, the year before my mother died. I was a fifteen-year-old girl, trying to act normal, and I'd saved up to buy a Valentine's Day card for my secret boyfriend Glenn. When it came to my father, I had no privacy whatsoever. He constantly checked my purse, my dresser drawers, and listened to my phone calls. After I bought the card I knew I had to find a place to hide it until I gave it to Glenn. I brought my social studies book home and hid the card between pages in the middle of the book. It was one of the mornings my mother was in the hospital.

"So," he said in a mocking tone, his face lit with a knowing sneer. "Did you get Glenny-Poo a Valentine's Day card?"

How did he know about Glenn, and how much did he know? I was afraid if I told him the truth he would have really beaten my ass, so I simply said, "No."

Then when we arrived at the school, I got out of his car, and all Hell broke loose. The card fell out of my book. He grabbed it before I could get to it and opened it.

"Get the fuck back in this car," he shouted, his face the color of a ripe tomato, rage flashing in his eyes. He began to beat me right in the school parking lot. He sped out of the lot and continued to punch me in the face all the way home while I huddled in the passenger seat crying. I was so terribly bruised, I couldn't even go to see my mother in the hospital or go to school for a whole week. When I finally did go back to school, I found out people in the parking lot saw this happening. But, no one said anything. As for my father, I never found out whether he was more mad at me for lying to him or because I defied him and got Glenn a Valentine's Day card instead of getting one for him.

Some of the witnesses said they knew my father was abused by his parents and had a horrible childhood. I could actually believe that, because my father's parents were always very scary to me. They were extremely strict, cold people and I recalled how I never wanted to spend any time with them.

My mother's parents were the exact opposite. They hugged us and played with us all the time. They lived across the street from our house, and during the time my mother was so sick, JoAnn and I lived with them for a while. I loved spending time at their house before they both passed away. I craved those normal times in my life like an addict craves drugs.

Even when I lived with my mother's parents, it didn't stop my father from demanding sex. I was able to sleep well at night because he wasn't there to paw me and rape me, but he'd make up excuses for me to go home with him during the day after school. Sometimes he'd take me into his bedroom and other times to the basement. After he was sexually satisfied, we went to the hospital to visit my mother.

When my beloved mother's father passed away, it devastated our family, especially my grandmother, mother, and brother.

That's when my father decided to build an extension onto my grandmother's house so we could live with her. He said when my mother was feeling better she could take care of my grandmother, who was quite ill by then. My grandfather always took such great care of her, and after he passed my grandmother was never the same. She died shortly after him, before the extension was even finished. We moved into her house anyway, and the Kossers lived right next door.

I thought about the Kossers during the hearing—Birdie, Big Mike, and their two kids—but was aware I was constantly being watched so I couldn't even let the hint of a smile escape.

As the testimonies continued, I choked up thinking about what a hard year that had been, and how grateful I was for the love they extended to us. I'd lost my favorite grandparents, my dog Cocoa, and my mother was deathly sick again, all within that same year.

For some reason I thought about the high tech alarm system my father installed in the new extension of the house while my mother was in the hospital. There was a keypad and motion detectors in the bedroom, and it showed where everyone was in the house at all times. One day Jimmy wasn't home, Mom was in the hospital, and JoAnn was hanging out with Birdie at her house. My father and I were alone.

"Cheryl, get in here," he called from his bedroom. I was really anxious that day. My mom wasn't doing that well and I just wanted to go to the hospital to see her. I couldn't understand how he could want to rape his daughter while his wife was in the hospital so close to death.

"Get in here, now!" When his voice took on that tone, you did what he said or paid the consequences. There was no question what he wanted. His nasty cigarette breath nauseated me as he grinned at me exposing stained yellow teeth. He came down on me with the full weight of his three hundred pound body, crushing me as always. I'd done the only thing I could. I covered my face with a pillow so I didn't have to smell his breath, shut my eyes, and let my mind take me somewhere else.

As yet another witness testified, practically calling him a saint, I clenched my fists in anger and struggled to keep my face as rigid as a stone. Meanwhile a vision of the weird thing that happened that day popped into my mind. He'd stopped moving all of a sudden. "Hello?" he yelled "HELLO, who's there?"

I took the pillow off my face and we both looked into the hallway. I'll never forget the skinny shadow of a man on the wall. The motion sensor didn't read any motion.

"Hello? Hello?" he continued to call.

No answer. He was so freaked out that he actually left me alone for a few days. In the car on the way to the hospital that day he said, "Did you see the shadow?"

"Yes, I think it was Grandpa."

"Your grandfather's dead. You think it was his ghost? Don't be ridiculous."

But the expression on his face gave him away. He believed it, too.

The second time it was my grandmother. When my mom was in the hospital, which felt like all the time, I was never able to spend too much time in my own bedroom because my father always demanded that I sleep in his bed.

In my own bedroom, a big headboard covered my bedroom window. There was no way you could move this queen size bed with its huge solid oak headboard. I used to be afraid if there ever was a fire I would be screwed. Sometimes I thought he covered my window so I would never be able to escape.

On this particular day my father was really mad at me and I was hanging out in my room. I felt the presence of my grandmother—just a shadow, but she looked beautiful to me. Not like the sick grandmother I remembered. She sat next to me on my bed. I did all the talking, but she did whisper, "You can't tell anyone I was here with you, Cheryl. If you do, I can't come back."

I wasn't sure if I was dreaming, but I don't think so. It was my bad luck that my father heard me talking to someone. I didn't have a phone in my room and cell phones didn't exist then. He came flying into my room, shouting, "Who were you talking to?"

I didn't say a word.

"I know someone is in here," he screamed, his face contorted in rage.

He looked under the bed, in my closet, and around my room. He was so angry that he grabbed me by my throat and shouted, "Who-the-fuck-were-you-talking-to? You better tell me or you'll be sorry."

I choked out, "Grandma. I was talking to Grandma."

He turned white and walked out of my bedroom. My grandmother never returned.

INCEST, MURDER AND A MIRACLE

◆ ◆ ◆

The hearing was a very long, stressful time in my life, but I was glad it was almost over. As it stretched on, I often thought, *Either way my life will have to be better.*

It may sound strange to someone who hasn't suffered what I did, but although I know I went on the stand to be questioned about my life and why I made the decisions I did, I must have blocked that part out completely because I don't remember much of it. However, I do remember being very scared and just staring at one person the whole time. I know I tried to answer questions in the best and most honest way I could.

I wasn't nervous about how I would answer because if you're not lying you won't have to worry about the prosecutor trying to trip you up. What I was worried about was that I would have to tell a room full of strangers everything that happened. I'd have to speak out loud to strangers about embarrassing, disgusting details of my life with my father. Thankfully, the prosecutor wasn't that hard on me. Mr. Gianelli told me later, "He doesn't want people to feel sorry for you, so he took it easy." That was perfectly fine with me.

The next hard part was the sentencing. Big Mike and Birdie drove me to the courthouse, and my brother came with us. It was a long drive to Riverhead and I knew it might be the last time I saw the sunlight for a very long time. All of my personal things were packed and placed in storage, and I steeled myself to receive whatever punishment they thought I deserved.

I was petrified and felt sick to my stomach but ready to get it over with. Before the judge made his decision, he asked me to stand and wanted to know if I had anything to say.

"I'm sorry. I'm sorry that any of this ever happened."

Then the decision was handed down—six months in jail and five years probation.

- 71 -

That's the last thing I remember. I guess I must have fainted because the next thing I was aware of was someone holding my arm really tight, saying, "Can you hear me?"

I managed to say, "Yes. Can I say goodbye to my family?"

The answer was a flat "No". I was taken directly to the Riverhead County Jail.

Chapter 12

CHERYL

IN JAIL

AFTER MY SENTENCE WAS HANDED DOWN, I was led away from the courthouse feeling numb and a little shell-shocked. I tried to comprehend the sentence I received—a term of six months jail time and five years' probation. It sounded like with good behavior and time already served, I would now only be incarcerated three and a half months.

I was definitely scared and upset that I had been sentenced to jail time. Considering I could have gotten up to fifteen years with the manslaughter charge, I also felt relieved it would only be three and a half months. I had already prepared myself for the possibility that I would have to do some time. My judge, Harvey Sherman, felt obligated to the public to make an example of me and my case. His reasoning was that if I received no jail time for my crime, every abuse victim would think there were no consequences for hiring someone to kill their abuser or even killing them themselves. I understood his reasoning to a point, but wondered if he ever considered the victim's side. Maybe if I'd gotten off, it would change the mind of some perpetrators, or at least make them think twice before abusing or raping anyone.

Maybe, just maybe, they would be afraid of the possibility of getting killed for doing harm to an innocent person.

Once I was inside the Riverhead County Jail I was taken for fingerprints and a mug shot. Then I was patted down by a female correctional officer. After she said, "Strip down," she proceeded to check my entire body for things I couldn't even imagine! I had just come from the courthouse, so I couldn't figure out why they thought I was hiding something, but these were the rules.

To make it through one hundred and six days in jail, I needed to start adjusting and do what I was told. I had to give up all my belongings except my bra and underwear. They gave me a shirt and pants which were dark evergreen prison attire. I would describe them as almost like medical scrubs except the material was a lot harder.

I had no socks because I had worn stockings with my dress for my sentencing. So there I was. This ugly, stiff prison suit with no socks and they gave me a used pair of shoes to wear from another inmate who had passed through. I was horrified.

Next I was given a tooth brush and a small tube of tooth paste, soap, a thin pillow, and a blanket. That was everything I had until my brother was able to bring my stuff from home the next day. He brought socks, sneakers, a brush, and thermal undergarments to wear under the harsh, stiff, itchy prison outfit. According to the rules, everything had to be new and in packaging so nothing could be hidden.

A correctional officer walked me through the hallway where I could hear all the other inmates. They were yelling so loud and chanting things that I tried to block out. I wasn't sure at that time which was worse—dealing with loud photographers and reporters or the inmates yelling things at me. I was very scared, but knew if I could handle my father, I could handle anyone or anything else I needed to.

Despite the awful things he did to me, there were some good

moments, so honestly, in some ways I did love my father. If I tried to fight him off, it was worse, so I learned to retreat into my own world. That might have been one of the reasons I didn't want to hurt or even kill him myself. I know that sounds strange because he was such an evil person, but I always wished he would just stop and we could have a normal father and daughter relationship. But these prisoners were strangers to me and I promised myself I would never let anyone else hurt me ever again without at least putting up a good fight.

So with those thoughts in my head I stayed close to the correctional officers walking me through the loud hallways until I got to the tier where my cell was located. They unlocked my cell and I saw it was a single cell, for which I was so grateful. You always see in the movies what it could be like, sharing a cell with other inmates who want to be *really* friendly with you. To my surprise and happiness I was alone. I walked in and just sat on the small metal single-frame bed on top of a thin mattress without a sheet.

That was the first time I heard the bars close. The sound echoed in my head and I knew this was the start of my new life. For years I had lived in an emotional prison located at 293 Magnolia Drive in Selden, and now a different prison behind bars in Suffolk County Riverhead Jail. Believe it or not I felt safe for the first time in my life behind those closed bars. A comfort that I had never really experienced in a long time. Locked up in my cell nobody could hurt me or force sex on me. I just needed to get through the nightmares and realize when I woke up, hopefully nobody would be hovering over me.

The hundred and six days had begun and I had to deal with learning to protect myself.

The toilet was next to my bed and everyone could see you do your business. The community shower in the hallway didn't have a curtain either—something that was hard for me because every male or female could pass in the hallway while you were in the shower and watch you. I had never really had privacy, but being nude in front of strangers, especially when you have always been ashamed of your body and felt so dirty already, was nerve wracking. I really felt exploited.

Jimmy eventually brought me flip flops to wear in the shower because I wouldn't go in there barefoot. Even so, I still didn't take very long showers. I always wore socks to bed and while in my cell. I decorated my cell with pictures of Rob from newspaper clippings by putting toothpaste on the back so they would stick to the cold concrete wall. One of the hardest parts was being away from him. I also hung cards I received from strangers, family, and friends.

I received a lot of nice gifts and a lot of very helpful, inspiring letters from many other sexually abused people who shared their stories with me. Their letters encouraged me to have strength and wished me luck. Those tons of letters got me through all the horrible days in jail because I answered every single person. Sadly, they were the ones who understood what it was like to be me.

Jimmy always put money in my jail account so I could purchase stamps and envelopes, and buy snacks that I shared with some of the friends I made. I did meet a couple of nice ladies who became my friends and were great support to me some of the days when I was really down. Even though I could get an hour-long visit every day from Rob, he also wrote to me every day. Jimmy and Rob never missed a visit, and they brought me gifts when they came. One of the gifts I appreciated the most was a headset and cassette player with some music. When I went to sleep or things got really loud with crazy people screaming, I could just put on my headphones and listen to the music that I'd missed hearing while I was in jail.

You would be surprised what you miss when everything

you've always had and taken for granted, like fresh air, good food and music, is taken away from you at any age, not just at eighteen.

It was really a hassle for Rob and Jimmy to visit me. They had to make an appointment in person to schedule a visit—this couldn't be done by telephone—and then they still had to wait in line a large part of the day. Rob and Jimmy went through the whole routine day in and day out because they knew how glad I was to see them. That was the great part. But there was a bad side, too. After the visit all inmates had to be strip-searched. I was traumatized during those searches and couldn't stop shaking every time a stranger inspected my private areas. As time went on, I became friendly with the correctional officers and they knew I was not there for drugs, so they weren't so aggressive with me.

As a young adult they placed me on a tier with mentally unstable inmates. They tried not to place us in a population with the harder criminals, but being with the mentally ill criminals wasn't easy either. While I was there, I heard and saw a lot of horrible things.

I was only eighteen and saw someone set themself on fire, someone try to hang themself with the bed sheet, and I constantly heard a lot of screaming and crying that lasted for hours. It was a scary place, and I will never understand how someone who did something that caused them to be there, would ever be stupid enough to do something else that lands them back in jail. I was allowed to go off my tier to do laundry and help serve food and mop the floors. When I was off tier, I met a lot of people and made friends with some of them. It kept me busy and the day went by faster until Rob and Jimmy came to visit.

I did have a bad experience with an inmate because the media insisted upon coming in and filming me in my cell without my permission. I tried to protest, but they said I had no choice because it was public property. So while they let the reporters stand outside of my tier and take pictures of me in my cell, I just sat on my bed and faced the wall so they couldn't see my face.

One inmate got really upset with me, thinking I was getting a lot of attention. She didn't want anyone to see her on the news, and I certainly didn't blame her. Anyway, we were allowed to go outside for thirty minutes a day to get fresh air and at last I felt comfortable enough to leave my cell and be with all of the inmate population. When I left my tier to mop and serve the food to the other inmates, they were in their tiers and didn't have access to me, so I felt safe doing those jobs.

Sure enough, she came over to me in the yard and began to yell at me and get in my face. After being beaten for so many years, I knew the signs all too well, and thought for sure she was going to hit me. Luckily the few friends I'd made came over and helped me. I was so scared that I didn't go out for days after that incident, but when I finally did, there were always friends who watched my back. In return when I got to serve the food, I gave them extra helpings. The food was really horrible, and I never wanted anything extra—I was lucky to finish a regular portion. I was thin already and I'd lost fifteen pounds, which was a lot for me, but I couldn't eat that food. All I thought of was going home. With that as my main focus, I got through the days.

Chapter 13

CHERYL

TRYING TO START MY NEW LIFE

AT LAST THE DAY HAD COME AND I was released from Riverhead County Jail on January 19, 1988. I was so excited that I'd finally be free after spending three and a half months in that hell hole, I could hardly contain myself. I was eighteen by then and looked forward to beginning my life with Rob.

They had arranged to release me very early in the morning so I wouldn't get bombarded by the media. To my surprise, Jimmy, Rob, and our best friend Craig picked me up in a white stretch limo. A limo! How incredible was that? I smiled so much that day, my cheeks hurt. Later, some reporters criticized me for looking happy as I rode in the limo, and all I can say to that is I guess it sold papers.

I was happy that so many people were on my side. For example, when we stopped for breakfast, the owners of the diner said, "No bill for you today. It's on the house. Just consider it a homecoming celebration."

There was a winter chill in the air, but the mere fact that I was able to breathe fresh air as a free woman filled me with joy.

As we drove along the tree-lined streets, I saw that Jimmy,

Rob, and Craig had placed yellow ribbons on all of the expressway signs and all the light poles. I had tried for an early release so I could spend Christmas with my family, and even though that was denied by Governor Cuomo, I made it though. When I saw all the ribbons and everyone's hard work to support me, my heart filled with overwhelming happiness.

Despite trying to evade them, members of the media did follow me to our second stop, which was Rob's family's house. Everyone was standing there in the driveway waiting to greet me. It was one of the happiest times in my life. I wore a white sweatshirt with my name on it that someone sent me while I was in jail. Sadly, everything I received while I was in jail came from the ones who understood what it was like to be me.

With the media watching, I said hello and gave everyone in the driveway a big hug, then went over to the huge oak tree in my future in-law's front lawn. They had wrapped it with a big yellow ribbon, and I cut it off.

The reporters bombarded me with questions.

"Cheryl, what are you going to do next?" one shouted as they jammed a mic in my face.

I said calmly, "I'm ready to start my new life and try to be the best wife and mother I can be. That's all I ever wanted."

That day Rob, the love of my life, proposed to me with a beautiful engagement ring. It had taken so many years, but my wish for the normal life every teenage girl dreams of was about to come true. That day, another big thing happened. I decided I would never allow anyone to hurt me in any way ever again. I had taken the first step in finding an inner strength I didn't know I had.

We set our wedding date for October 9, 1988. I needed to focus on going to probation, trying to find a job, and then the good stuff—planning our wedding in nine months. But, I desperately needed sleep. Although I was free now, the nightmares still tormented me every night. They do until this day.

A couple of days after I was released, I went skiing for a few days with Rob, Jimmy, and his girlfriend. We needed to get away from all the media, just get to know each other again and be able to spend some time together.

When we got back home, we were given a beautiful engagement party and that summer Rob's parents gave me an awesome bridal shower. After everything I'd experienced, I had to get used to being able to have fun spending time with our family and friends whom I hadn't seen in a while. Everyone gave us great gifts to start our new lives. I hoped it wasn't a dream.

During the months leading up to our wedding, we were still trying to work and save for our life together. Rob's parents paid for a storybook wedding and it was one of the best days of my life. I will forever be grateful for all the love and support they had given us. We couldn't have gone through any of this without Rob's amazing family.

Jimmy bought my stunning wedding gown and I truly felt like a princess for the first time in my life. I had finally experienced a glimpse of what it felt like not to feel shameful or dirty—what it was like to actually feel that maybe I did deserve to be a princess.

Deacon Bob is still a big part of our family. He performed our wedding ceremony and baptized both of our daughters. When my sister got married, he also performed JoAnn's wedding ceremony at the Stony Brook Duck Pond. I have never been able to love or trust many people in my life, but Deacon Bob is one of the few.

Paul Gianelli is also a very important person to me. Paul and his wife, Linda, came to our wedding and we have been constant friends. Many years have passed, but we try to visit every once in a while.

Jimmy said he would be honored to walk me down the aisle and for that short moment it was just Jimmy and me again, depending upon each other and protecting each other, the way we used to when we were younger. I walked proud, with my head held high, not minding that people were taking pictures of me. It was one of the best days of my life!

If my brother hadn't walked me down the aisle, I would have asked Paul, because although I would have wanted to ask my father-in-law, Liz had always been "Daddy's Little Girl." I didn't want to chance taking the honor of being the first to be walked down the aisle by her father away from her. My father was anything but a great example of being a dad, and I consider my father-in-law my dad. He taught me what a real father is and how to be able to love and trust a man again without having to give anything back in return. I couldn't have gone through a lot of things without him helping me. I adore him with all my heart.

We danced to the song "Through the Years" at our wedding and every time I hear that song, I think of him and cry with happiness.

I was nineteen when I became Mrs. Robert C. Cuccio. I thanked God to finally be rid of the Pierson last name. Even on that day the media tried to follow us in the limo and tried to come into the reception hall to get some pictures, but our family put a kibosh on that. This was our spectacular day to rejoice, and damn the media.

INCEST, MURDER AND A MIRACLE

Sympathy for Cheryl

Her day in jail

By ▓▓▓▓▓▓
and ▓▓▓▓▓▓▓▓

Cheryl Pierson, now inmate No. 45709, got a taste of jail routine yesterday with sympathetic support from many fellow prisoners.

Pierson, 18, is assigned to Cell 5 on the first floor of Minors North, a section for 16-to-19-year-olds in the Suffolk County Correctional Facility in Riverhead, L.I. She was jailed Monday on a six-month sentence for her role in the 1986 contract killing of her father.

"I think she's a nice girl," said a prisoner in Cell 4. "She said she feels guilty for what she did and knows it was wrong. She told me this last night. She said she wants to straighten out her life when she gets out."

Pierson, who testified that her father sexually abused her, is in a 6 by 8-foot cell. Her spare set of olive-drab

Girl Due in Court In Dad's Killing

By ▓▓▓▓▓▓▓▓▓▓

Seven months ago, on an icy February morning, Joseph Pierson, a 42-year-old widower, was found shot dead on the driveway of his Selden home. Eight days later, his daughter Cheryl, a popular 16-year-old high school cheerleader, was charged with hiring a classmate to kill him.

Tomorrow, after several delays on the part of prosecutors and defense attorneys, the murder case that received publicity across the country will go to court.

A pre-trial hearing is scheduled for 9:30 a.m. at State Supreme Court in Riverhead, where Justice Harvey Sherman will hear arguments on statements given to police by Cheryl Pierson, who allegedly said she wanted her father dead because he was sexually abusing her, and by Sean Pica, the Coram youth who is accused of carrying out the contract-killing. Both have pleaded innocent to second-degree murder and conspiracy, and face penalties up to 25 years-to-life in prison if convicted. After the hearing, the trial is expected to start, although it could be delayed by legal maneuvering.

Pierson's attorney contends that she was

Cheryl Pierson

a desperate victim of incest; Pica's attorney maintains that his client's statement was coerced in a grueling four-hour session while his mother searched frantically for her son.

Interviews with the two teenagers, family members and friends after Joseph Pierson's death produced conflicting perceptions of a man who was characterized by some as a tough-talking, devoted father and by others as an overly harsh disciplinarian. His wife, Cathleen, had died of kidney ailment a year before his death. His son, James, 19, whose rock-star ambitions and appearance irritated his father, moved out of the house later that year.

Pierson and Pica told police that the first talked about killing Joseph Pierson in November, when a Mastic woman, Beverly Wallace, was charged with the contract killing of her husband, police said. Suffolk County Court judge, declaring that testimony showed John Wallace was "despicable, inhumane, an animal," ruled last week that Beverly Wallace should not go to jail for his death. But the men convicted of carrying out John Wallace's murder received stiff prison sentences.

Any effect that decision may have on the Pierson-Pica case is a matter of conjecture. Pica's attorney, Martin Efman, defended the gunman in the Wallace case. "It was a different situation," Efman said because "there was no relationship" between his client and the Wallace family. He said that Cheryl and Sean "at best were very friendly, at worst, schoolmate
—Continued on Page 2

TUESDAY, SEPTEMBER 16, 1986 · 7

Incest is cited in patricide case

Teen said she wanted to protect sister

▓▓▓▓▓▓▓▓

RIVERHEAD, N.Y. — Cheryl Pierson wiped away ▓▓▓ tears Monday as a detective testified she confessed to having her father killed because of repeated sexual abuse.

"She said her father did everything sexual to her," Detective K. James McCready said at a pretrial hearing on the admissibility of evidence.

He said the 17-year-old former cheerleader confessed to enlisting classmate Sean Pica to kill her father because she feared he would sexually assault her sister, JoAnn, 9.

Pica, a 17-year-old Eagle scout and son of a policeman and a catechism teacher, is accused of shooting James Pierson with a .22-caliber rifle.

Pierson, 42, an electrician, was found dead outside his Selden, N.Y. home Feb. 5.

Pica has contended that he agreed to accept $1,000 for the slaying, but received only $400 from Cheryl's boyfriend, Robert Cuccio, 18, police said.

Cuccio was charged with conspiracy. Cheryl and Pica were charged with second-degree murder and conspiracy.

McCready said Cheryl told police her father's advances started in 1979, after her mother was diagnosed as having a rare kidney disease. Cathleen Pierson died Feb. 13, 1985.

Outside the courtroom, Mer-

PIERSON: Sobs on her way to a court appearance

supports his sister, stood away from their grandmother, Virginia Pierson. She believes Cheryl may have had her distortion father killed for his $36,000 insurance policy.

A shoving match between James and a photographer developed as a sobbing Cheryl hid under James' arm. "Get that camera off my head!" she yelled at a TV cameraman.

When Pica takes the stand today or on Wednesday, his lawyer will contend that his confession was coerced. "There is an allegation of a pistol being placed on his head," said lawyer Martin Efman.

Cheryl's lawyer, Paul Gianelli and his defense will rely on evidence of family and friends, and therapists who will discuss "the horror of incest."

- 83 -

Real-life roles: Robert Cuccio Jr. and Cheryl Pierson, above, on the day she left jail and got engaged; her father, James Pierson Sr.; and, below, their TV counterparts, Heather Fairfield, David Schwimmer and Charles Haid.

Attorney Paul Gianelli, above with Pierson in 1986; below, they're portrayed by Mike Farrell and Fairfield.

Cheryl Pierson found a way to make sure her father would never sexually abuse her again.

INCEST, MURDER AND A MIRACLE

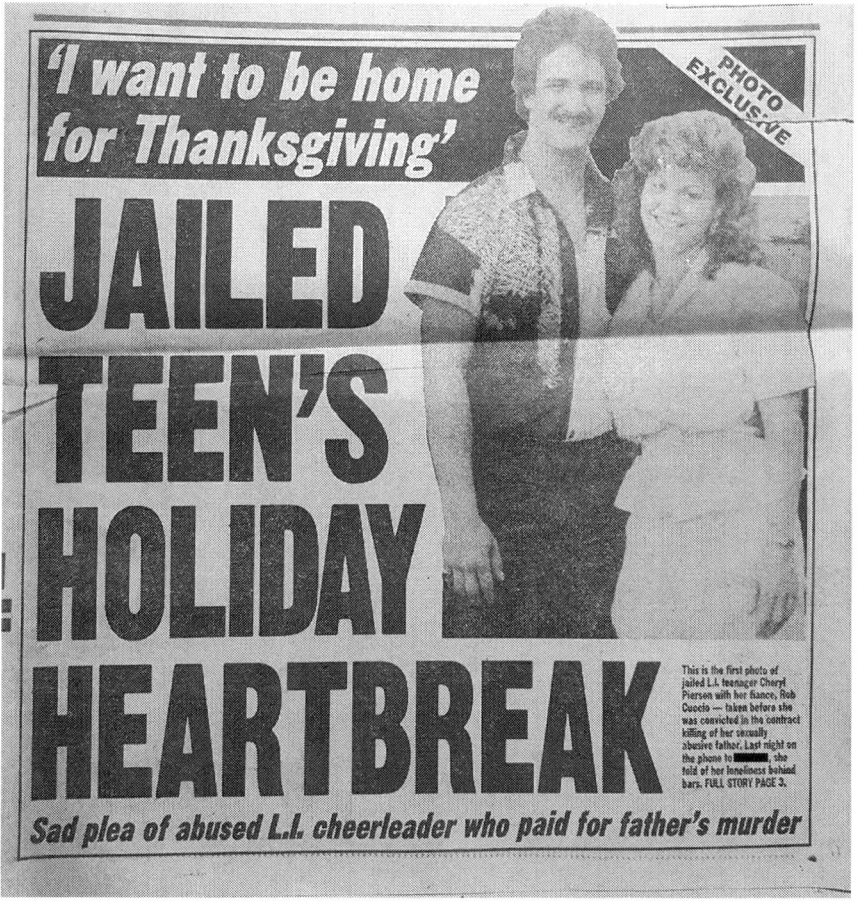

'I want to be home for Thanksgiving'

JAILED TEEN'S HOLIDAY HEARTBREAK

PHOTO EXCLUSIVE

This is the first photo of jailed L.I. teenager Cheryl Pierson with her fiance, Rob Cuocco — taken before she was convicted in the contract killing of her sexually abusive father. Last night on the phone to ███████, she told of her loneliness behind bars. FULL STORY PAGE 3.

Sad plea of abused L.I. cheerleader who paid for father's murder

- 85 -

Chapter 14

CHERYL

SETTING THE RECORD STRAIGHT

AS PART OF WRITING THIS BOOK, I HAD to force myself to read the copy of Dena Kleiman's 1988 book about me and my case, *A Deadly Silence,* that I've kept out of sight in a secret place for many years. After finally suffering through reading it cover-to-cover, accompanied by many tears as I tried not to go into meltdown, at least I finally know what was actually in it. When it first came out, I'd only gotten through twenty-seven pages and couldn't go any farther because of the anger and hurt that consumed me.

In my opinion, she should have been ashamed of herself for exploiting a teenager for profit. Through the things she fabricated and falsehoods she repeated in print, she made my life even worse than it already was by presenting incorrect information as truth.

I must admit it feels good to be able to set the record straight at last. I feel she did me and other abuse victims such a great dis-service by inventing information that supposedly came directly from me.

What I've written in this chapter is drawn from only two

pages of her book. Imagine how much there would be if I challenged everything. It's entirely possible other abuse victims were afraid to come forward after reading her book or watching the TV movie based on the book because of the way everything was portrayed.

Did she not realize that thousands of abuse victims are reluctant to seek help because they know they will probably become the accused? I hope by telling the truth in my book, it will give them courage to speak up. In the aftermath of the murder and my pre-sentencing hearing, so many who were convinced I made everything up validated their opinion by asking, "Why didn't she tell anyone what was going on while it was happening?"

Of course the answer to that is the person is afraid of their abuser and that they won't be believed. Besides that, however, is the injustice of books like *A Deadly Silence.* Unfortunately, people believe what they read in print, and books that illustrate how victims can become even more victimized when fabricated information is presented as fact only makes them more fearful. That is why it is so important to build awareness of the reality of abuse so victims are not afraid to speak out.

Dena Kleiman knew very little about the real me and what my life actually was like, so my supposed likes, dislikes, thoughts and many of the incidents were entirely off base.

I can't address every wrong thing in that book, but since pages twenty-six and twenty-seven were my stumbling block, here are two questions that kept going through my mind as I read:

How dare she put words into my mouth and thoughts in my head, then make them all seem like reality? How could she even write a book like this about someone she only spoke to for a very short time under very stressful circumstances with my lawyer present. I only gave that interview because he thought it was best to get her on our side since she was already writing such negative information about me in the New York Times.

I can't go back and change what was written, but I will tell you the truth. I'm certain she wouldn't have made up some of the things she did if only she had taken the time to understand me. I was a frightened teenager who didn't feel comfortable with trusting a complete stranger and telling her intimate details of my life in the cold harsh way she asked me questions for her newspaper articles. Maybe she would have questioned unconfirmed information she got from other people who weren't very fond of me for their own reasons, and wouldn't have written their lies as though they were the truth. Unfortunately that didn't happen and she made it seem like she knew me and everything about me.

One of the statements that hurt the most was, *"...a teenager who seemed destined to have everything she wanted."* It might have seemed like that on the surface, but before condemning me and making it seem I created my own problems, shouldn't she have checked out what my life truly was like?

That statement made it sound like I had a wonderful life filled with a great family and received anything I asked for. Sort of like being born with the proverbial "silver spoon in my mouth." Thinking about my own daughters, I would hope that they have dreams and goals about having everything good in their lives. All children should want to achieve goals in their lives and shouldn't have to include hoping their loved ones don't ever hurt them.

Even young Cheryl Pierson had hopes, dreams and goals. Is that a bad thing? After all, would I have wanted to watch my mother become very ill when I was only eleven and die by the time I was fifteen? What about losing both my loving grandparents whom I lived with for a short while when my mom first became sick, or watching my childhood dog die after my father kicked her so hard? Would I have wanted to see my brother getting beaten on a regular basis? Hardly.

The life where I supposedly got anything I wanted consisted of learning on my own how to wash everyone's clothes, cook dinner for the family, clean the whole house, and take care of my two-year-old sister who was eight years younger than me. And, oh yes, despite all of that responsibility, go to school and get decent grades while being made to have sex with my own father on a regular basis. Sounds like that little girl got anything she wanted, doesn't it?

"Cheryl was an average student. She never did much better than B. She had little interest in reading, mathematics or current affairs."

Makes me sound like a total airhead, right? So let's talk about that. Dr. Nancy Stalick, Professor of Philosophy, UFC, states,

"B = Far above average, fully meets average understanding as evidenced in course work and fully understands the basics and can deal with concepts somewhat beyond that level." According to her chart on https://pegasus.cc.ucf.edu, "C = Average, meets minimum expectations and satisfies course requirements."

I received a lot of B's and some A's, but I worked hard for them. That's not average. With the problems I had at home, some days I was lucky I was able to function and get out of bed at all. And believe you me, the only reason I was able to do that was because it was my only escape from the hell I lived in. Even if my father wouldn't have gone berserk if I came home with an average report card, in reality what would have been wrong if I actually had gotten Cs?

As for her claim that I had little interest in reading, math and current affairs, how would she know that without knowing me? Unlike most kids, I didn't get much time to do those things because I was constantly busy taking care of a family, responsible for maintaining a household and every other chore including satisfying my father's sick desires. So yes, maybe I didn't get to enjoy reading but that doesn't mean I didn't have an interest in doing it. As for being up to speed with current affairs, that's funny because every night at six o'clock I had to listen to the news during dinner time. I wasn't allowed to watch television while I ate, so I just listened to it. I was pretty knowledgeable about current affairs and the news. If not, I might never have heard about the Beverly Wallace case.

According to the book, "She talked to her friends for hours about love songs she liked on the radio, boys she had crushes on in school, dreams about the kind of house she would live in one day, the kind of wedding she would have."

First I must clarify that I did not have hours to spend with friends because they weren't allowed at my house nor was I allowed to go out very often. I'm not sure where the "for hours" came into play. I didn't spend those supposed hours on the phone, because I barely had enough hours to take care of the house I lived in, so dreaming about another house or getting married to take care of a husband when I didn't even want to be touched is such a far cry from how I really felt.

Of course, I wanted my life to be better and have a husband who would protect me, take care of me and not hurt me. Who wouldn't? It is so maddening to me that she would say such a thing. There wasn't much room in my mind for it to be filled with love songs, bridesmaids dresses, the house I would live in and how I would scheme and plan to bump into boys I liked. Most of my thoughts were about survival.

Her book made it sound like I had all these opportunities and messed them up for myself. Not quite the way it was! Having everything I wanted definitely was not my destiny.

At least she got it right when she said I never smoked, did drugs or wore revealing clothes. My life was so out of control, I would never allow myself to lose more control by doing drugs. I already felt powerless, so that was not an option and I'm still the same way to this day.

"Cheryl Pierson still slept with a teddy bear at night."

The only bear I slept with was a three-hundred pound over-weight, cigarette-smelling bad-tempered asshole called my father. And that wasn't by choice.

"She was still unclear on how babies were born."

Really! I probably knew more about sex and babies than people twice my age. If people wanted to say bad things about me because they loved him, didn't believe me about the sexual abuse and were upset he had been murdered, I completely understand their bias.

I lay my head down to sleep at night with a clear conscience because I know I wasn't the person I was painted to be. My father, God and I knew the truth.

I'm not sure if Dena Kleiman has her own children, but I suspect she doesn't because of the comments she made about me in her book. Any person who is truly a mother would never speculate about a teenage girl like she did or write what I view as the garbage she wrote about me. It was important to me to write this chapter in my book because it is time for me to try to release the hurt and anger I have kept within me for nearly thirty years.

Chapter 15

CHERYL

BITTERSWEET—MY SISTER JOANN

JOANN WAS JUST TWO YEARS OLD WHEN my mother became sick, too young to be aware of what I dealt with on a daily basis. From the time I was ten my mission in life was to protect her.

After our father was murdered, she chose not to live with me at Birdie and Big Mike's house, but stayed with her Aunt Marilyn, my father's sister. During that time, her mind was poisoned against me and we had very little communication. As young as I was, I had been a mother to her and her anger toward me really hurt. As the years went on, it only got worse.

I had never given up on the idea that maybe someday we would be together as loving sisters again. Seven years had passed, but I'd always let her know where I lived, just in case she needed me. She was fifteen when she just showed up at our front door one day, saying she ran away from her aunt's house and wanted to stay with us.

For years after I was released from jail so many people asked me why I decided to stay in New York, so close to Selden. It was a reasonable question since my problems and troubles were far from over. If I was in a store, people pointed at me and made no secret of the fact that they were whispering about me. Others threw things at me, ran cars into my house, and broke my front windows. Then there was my fear whenever Sean's friends tried to run me off the road.

I endured all of it because in my heart I knew someday JoAnn would need me and I wanted be there for her. That meant I had to be where she could find me easily. Just as Birdie promised my mother on her death bed that she would take care of us kids, I promised my mother I would always take care of JoAnn—always be there for her. I've never broken that promise and it is as strong today as the day I made it.

I knew I'd made the right decision when I opened the door and saw her standing there. Happiness surged through me, but I soon discovered it wasn't going to be a bed of roses. It was clear that she was still very angry with me. There were so many unresolved issues to be worked out, and I knew that wasn't going to be easy.

We hadn't spoken to each other in years. I'd never had the chance to tell her my side of the story, so I don't know if she even believed me when I said, "I did it because I had to protect you from our father at all costs. I have paid a very big price for that, but I kept you safe."

JoAnn had been heavily brainwashed by our father's side of the family. During the seven years she lived with them, they filled her young head with lies about me rather than admit what a monster my father was. When she chose not to come with me to Birdie and Big Mike's house, but to stay with my aunt, I'd always felt it was because she hated me. After we finally talked to each other, I learned she not only had been programmed to hate me, but was actually afraid of me because of all the lies she was fed.

If only I'd been able to tell her the truth at the time, but I felt she was too young to understand what was in store for her had I not protected her. No child should ever endure what I did.

Maybe when she came to me that day she knew and remembered the love I had for her and how I'd cared for her when she was younger. I hoped she understood that I would never hurt her. As young as I'd been, she was still more like my child than my sister. Even when she heard it during the hearing, I think she was too young to understand what sexual abuse meant. Therefore, because all of the lies that were told to her year after year, even when she was old enough to understand what it was, I don't think she ever believed her father raped me. The best I could hope for was for her to know I did love her with all my heart.

Rob and I were still a young couple when she came to me. I was just twenty-three and Rob was twenty-five. We assumed all of the expense and responsibility for my sister. My father had tried to buy me because of all the awful things he did to me in secret. It is said that sometimes we repeat the sins of our parents, and I found myself doing the same thing—I tried to buy her love. Even though I'd done what I'd believed I had to do to make sure he could never hurt her like he'd hurt me, I felt guilty for the pain I had caused her by taking her dad from her. That might sound irrational, but you must realize he hadn't hurt her yet and she didn't believe anything I said.

I became her legal guardian and Rob and I took care of her to the best of our ability. Sam was just one year old and it was quite a job raising both of them. After all the years spent hating me, some days JoAnn became very angry and said extremely hurtful things. She didn't trust me, and made it obvious. In addition to just being a teenage girl, many issues hovered over us throughout the years she lived with us because of what she had been led to believe about me.

After a while I thought maybe she ran away from her strict aunt because she thought she would have no rules at my house. Well, she was wrong about that. I had taken care of her a good part of her life, but no matter what I tried I couldn't seem to get her to give me the respect I knew I deserved. She got along well with Rob but not with me, and that truly hurt my feelings.

I made so many sacrifices for her, but when it came to her respecting me she often acted like a nasty teenage bitch instead. Now I realize part of that behavior is merely a stage many teenage girls go through, but she continued to throw roadblocks in the way of my loving her and taking care of her.

Our father was an electrician and did a lot of side work using materials that belonged to the company he worked for. Those jobs were pure profit. In addition to everything else, he owned a company that sold cable boxes. My brother repaired them and I cleaned them. One thing I will say for my father—he knew how to make a buck and was definitely a hard worker. He also had a talent for investing his money for the greatest returns. If there is anything good I can say about him, it's that he gave Jimmy and me a good work ethic.

On the other hand, with his nasty temper and little bit of power, even adults were afraid of him.

He always had his hand in something and those ventures were very profitable, so there was a lot of money in our father's estate when he died. For example, he had a couple of side businesses that included buying and fixing up cars, trucks, and motorcycles. He gave Jimmy and me the task of cleaning and detailing all the vehicles, then sold them for a profit. He also loaned money to people at high interest rates like a loan shark. He had a couple of rental houses and more investments I didn't even know about.

When JoAnn was eighteen she received a good deal of money from his estate. As for me, I'd received nothing because I signed over my rights to prove that I didn't want him killed for the money as so many people claimed. That was fine with me because I looked at his dirty money as bad karma money.

Sometimes things work out in a strange way. You don't go

through everything I did without it leaving scars, and I couldn't have made it through without therapy. When my sister got her money, she paid for my therapist bills. I told myself it seemed fair that his money pay for my therapy because he was the reason I needed it. If I'd had a normal life, it would have been much different.

Although JoAnn and I had various issues over those years, we had a lot of good times, too. Rob and I threw a huge Sweet Sixteen party for her at a nice hotel/restaurant and tried to make a big deal for her senior prom. She looked like a princess for both.

After she graduated from high school she met a nice boy named Charlie. We found out JoAnn and Charlie were expecting a baby, but he was going away to serve our country. They decided to get married before he left, so Rob and I put together a beautiful wedding at the Stony Brook Duck Pond followed by dinner at a local restaurant. It was a magical day. While Charlie was in the service, we threw a baby shower in our backyard and my sister received all the things she would need to take care of her new beautiful angel.

I was in the delivery room with JoAnn on August 18, 1997, to catch a beautiful baby girl, Daisy Cathleen. Daisy is like our third daughter and is as close to our girls as sisters could be. Unfortunately, Charlie and JoAnn's marriage didn't work out, but we were lucky that Charlie decided he would bring Daisy back to Long Island after his tour was up in the service.

Daisy lives with him while JoAnn decided to stay in California. Charlie is a great father and allowed our family to spend a lot of quality time with her as our girls grew up. JoAnn has since had two more amazing children, Alex and Jake. Although we love them to death, we don't get to see them as much because JoAnn still lives in California.

My sister finally knows what it's like to love, protect, and take care of someone other than herself.

She has grown into a wonderful person and we love and respect each other, which is what I always dreamed of. One of the best parts is that she finally told me she does believe everything I have told her and is sorry it all happened. Sometimes she has a hard time facing setbacks, as we all do, but she tries hard. Even now, it is a learning process for all of us.

Chapter 16

CHERYL

SIGNS OF TROUBLE

WE BOTH SAT THERE IN THE COURTROOM, so confident our case was being proven beyond a doubt. Jurors listened as the testimony went on, and my thoughts wandered to how Rob had always been very healthy, but for the six months before disaster struck he had mentioned now and then that he didn't feel very good.

He complained of pain in the left side of his chest, shortness of breath, and numbness in his left arm. Because Rob had been a registered nurse for the past seventeen years, he was very aware that these were not symptoms to be ignored.

Although he played flag football for about twenty years, after retiring from his team to coach Casey's softball team, he hadn't played for three years. Now that she would be in college, he wanted to play again but was a little concerned about the chest pains, shortness of breath, and numb left arm, so he decided to go to a primary physician to get a physical.

Well, he hadn't gotten a physical for many years. When I questioned why he felt he needed a physical now, he said, "It's nothing to worry about. I just think it's a good idea to confirm

INCEST, MURDER AND A MIRACLE

everything is okay before I start to play again."

Working in an outpatient oncology center and a hospital as well, he was always surrounded by doctors. If he had something wrong, they generally took care of whatever the minor issue was. This wasn't some minor thing they could prescribe medication for or put a Band Aid on. Because it had been so long since he'd seen a doctor outside of those in his office, he had to find a new primary physician.

In December 2011, Rob went to his new doctor and described his symptoms. She immediately took an EKG in the office and a medical history. Then she told Rob she didn't like what she heard or saw and to see a cardiologist as soon as possible for a cardiac workup.

The next day Rob made an appointment to see Dr. Mercurio, a cardiologist across the plaza in the medical complex where he worked. When he called the office, he told the receptionist that after his primary doctor took an EKG, she said he needed an echo-cardiogram.

Dr. Mercurio's office was convenient and Rob didn't have to take much time off for an appointment, so he didn't check out other cardiologists. During the first visit, besides taking a medical history, Dr. Mercurio also took another EKG, although Rob brought the one taken by his primary doctor. Then he ordered an echocardiogram to be done at a later date and charged a fifty dollar copayment. When the echocardiogram was taken in January 2012, Dr. Mercurio read it as normal.

Rob said, "It might be normal, but I still have all of the symptoms, so something must be causing them."

Dr. Mercurio ordered a nuclear stress test, said to come back in a few days to get the test done, and added that there would be another fifty dollar copayment.

We thought everything was set for the test, but the day before it was scheduled Rob received a phone call from the

- 99 -

doctor's office. "United Healthcare/Oxford has denied the request for the nuclear stress test, but we still want you to come in for an echo stress test."

Rob may be a registered nurse, but cardiology is not his specialty, so he asked, "Is the echo stress test as good as the nuclear stress test?"

The person who called said, "Yes, it's just as good."

Rob was no stranger to insurance companies denying tests. He told me it seems like insurance companies deny every test the doctors want, but his office generally follows up and says the test is essential and has to be approved. Approval usually doesn't take more than fifteen minutes.

Apparently this wasn't the procedure in Dr. Mercurio's office. So the following day they performed the echo stress test, and Dr. Mercurio assured Rob he would be able to tell if something was wrong with his heart.

When he came home, Rob told me the test was grueling and he had a hard time finishing it because he was so short of breath. He added with a grimace, "But they made sure to collect another fifty dollars."

When the doctor called with the results the next day, he said, "Everything was fine and everything looks good. Continue to take your blood pressure medicine along with Lipitor, exercise, eat better, and quit smoking."

Rob even cut down to four or five cigarettes a day over the next few weeks, but to his dismay he still wasn't feeling any better. The shortness of breath, chest pain, and numbness hadn't gone away. As time went by, I wondered whether he was still having the pains but had stopped telling me. He later said, "I felt like I was crying wolf and maybe it was all in my head and nothing was wrong. After all, the doctor assured me everything was normal every time I saw him."

One day at the end of April we were both at work when I received a panicked cell phone call from Rob late in the afternoon. He was sitting outside of his office and was very upset, nervous, and it sounded like he was almost crying. This was totally unlike my husband.

He said, "Cheryl, I have horrible pressure on my chest. I can't breathe and I'm diaphoretic." Diaphoretic meant he was sweating. He continued, "Before I went outside to cool off and get some fresh air, one of my coworkers, Nicole, said I didn't look good and insisted upon taking my blood pressure. It was180/120, and that's not good, but I convinced her I was okay and just needed some air."

Then he said he decided to call me while he was outside. I tried to get in touch with my boss to ask her if I could leave work to go check on him, but I couldn't get in touch with her. He said, "Don't worry about it, the pain has started to subside."

Nicole came outside to get Rob because the doctor in his office wanted to take a look at him. He took Rob's blood pressure again and it was a little lower than before. By the time they got him another blood pressure pill and an aspirin from the pharmacy in the same complex, about twenty-five minutes had passed before they took an EKG.

It was decided not to take him to the emergency room but he had to agree to see his cardiologist the next day. The doctor in Rob's office called Dr.Mercurio himself and discussed his concerns about what happened with Rob earlier. He was able to get Rob the earliest appointment they had at eleven-thirty the next day.

I thought back to how I'd just about been ready to leave work to come to his office when Rob called me. "You don't have to come. I'm feeling quite a bit better and I have an appointment to see Dr. Mercurio tomorrow morning."

I honestly have to admit at that point I wondered if he really was having chest pain. I told myself that it could be heartburn or

- 101 -

something totally different. Otherwise, how could this keep happening, and yet nobody was really taking it seriously.

Rob kept his appointment the next day as scheduled and brought the EKG the doctor in his office had taken the day before. When he handed it to Dr. Mercurio, he said, "I thought I was having a heart attack yesterday. The pain was awful, I couldn't breathe, and I was covered in sweat."

The doctor began to laugh. "You didn't have a heart attack. My guess is that it was nothing but an anxiety attack."

The only thing that was resolved was that Rob owed another fifty dollar copay, and the doctor's attitude convinced him that maybe it really wasn't chest pain. That day Rob called me from the parking lot while walking back to his office, and he was fuming. "Cheryl, can you believe it? This guy said it was anxiety and to come back in three weeks for a blood pressure check. He said just continue to take my meds and to quit smoking. You know I'm doing that already. I swear, that was no anxiety or f***ing panic attack."

I've often thought about that day in view of everything that happened later and wonder why as two pretty smart people we didn't go for a second opinion. I guess our problem was that with Rob being in the medical field for eighteen years and me working in an ER for over seven years, we both trusted doctors. If only that had been our first mistake.

While waiting the three years for our malpractice case to be heard, I asked myself that question over and over. Why didn't we get a second opinion? I thought I'd finally figured it out.

My mother had gotten very sick when I was just ten years old. She also had gone to the doctor and they misdiagnosed her for at least six months. It wasn't until my father brought her to Downstate Medical Center in the Bronx that she was finally diagnosed with a rare blood disease that was deteriorating her organs and put her into kidney failure. My mother underwent two

- 102 -

kidney transplants in the five years of her illness, but our family loved and trusted the second doctor and all the nurses who had taken good care of my mom. I guess that's the part I chose to remember, and not the part about the first doctor who screwed up.

A week and a half had gone by, and Rob seemed to be okay, so I told myself maybe it really was anxiety. Then Rob finally told me the symptoms were still there, but he had decided not to tell anyone anymore, and cautioned me not to tell anyone about his chest pain under any circumstances. My second mistake.

I decided to tell his mother just a little bit because deep down I still felt something was wrong and needed to talk about it. My mother-in-law called her daughter, Liz, and Liz called Rob to talk to him about it. Rob was very upset with me and from then on he didn't tell me anything about his continuing symptoms. Maybe if I hadn't said anything, he would have let me know how bad it was getting.

We had been together for twenty-eight years by that time. All through my mother's death, my father's murder, the court cases, the birth and raising of our two beautiful daughters, family issues, our ups and downs, my nightmares—whatever the issues were, we always had each other to fall back on. We know each other better than we know ourselves and yet, for the first time in our lives together, Rob didn't tell me he still didn't feel well and maybe had even gotten a little worse.

When I was young, and still my father's victim, it was often denial that got me through. Some habits die hard, and I sometimes think maybe I did know Dr. Mercurio was wrong but I was in denial. Maybe I couldn't face the thought of my husband being sick.

I had lost so much in my life already. The only family I have left are our daughters, Rob, and his family, Jimmy and JoAnn, and our best friends AnnMarie and James. Having the issues I had while growing up, I never had many childhood friends or family members who stayed by my side. We grew up trusting very few people, and those few became our inner circle. Believe me, when you go through any kind of tragedy, you really find out who your friends are. That's a life lesson learned the hard way. You learn what to complain about and what to cherish.

Chapter 17

CHERYL

A NIGHTMARE

MAY 13, 2012. MOTHER'S DAY WAS a beautiful, sunny day in Suffolk County, Long Island, where we have lived all our lives. Despite the lovely weather, I felt a twinge of sadness because Mother's Day is a constant reminder that my mother died so young.

Still, I always put on my happy face and do my best to celebrate the day for my two girls. Samantha was twenty and Casey seventeen. It's also a way for me to honor my mother-in-law who had been in my life for the past twenty-seven years and given me a mother's love.

As I was getting dressed, I thought about everything Rob and I have been through before, during, and since my trial—it's so much more than an average couple would endure in a lifetime. Rob's sister, Liz, and his brother-in-law, Scott, were making the dinner that year and our first stop was at my in-laws' house. Neither of them were very healthy by then and they needed help to get out of the house.

We've had a standing rule for many years that if Liz, who is two years older than Rob, makes a holiday dinner, Rob and I pick

- 105 -

up Mom and Dad, and vice versa. His brother Tony, who is eight years younger, lives out of state. The holiday dinners are always on Long Island, so Tony generally isn't included in the driving or hosting plans. We're just happy when he's able to come.

That Mother's Day I was looking forward to using the new camera Rob gave me for Christmas and thought this would be a great opportunity. You know how sometimes you feel compelled to do something, but have no idea why? Tony was at that dinner, too, which was rare, and I kept snapping pictures of my mother-in-law with all three of her children and all the grandchildren with their grandparents. I shot so many photos I was sure we would have a good one for our next Christmas card. I remember being driven by this compulsion to keep snapping and I couldn't stop. Even if they didn't say it out loud, I imagined them thinking "Enough, already," but I kept snapping.

Who knows? Maybe a higher power was guiding me to do that. If Rob hadn't survived his massive heart attack only hours after we returned home, those pictures would have been the last pictures we ever had of all of us together.

When my father-in-law began to look tired, we knew it was time to take him home.

He weighs over three-hundred pounds and suffers from Parkinson's disease, so taking him out is no easy task. We always needed two vehicles to accommodate everyone. I had driven my in-laws home and Rob followed in his truck. He had to help his father into the house and upstairs to his bedroom, which meant partially carrying him. It was lot of work but neither of us minded doing it.

It was still light when we got home and Rob said, "I think I'll mow the lawn before it gets dark."

For the past few years we had a lawn service because we were always so busy on weekends. Rob coached our youngest daughter Casey's softball team—something he really enjoyed. We traveled with her on weekends, and as any softball player's parents would agree, when your child is on different teams it's almost necessary to have a lawn service. Rob was in the process of trying to quit smoking, a habit he'd had from the time he was fifteen, and the gardeners had gotten expensive. Although he had vowed to quit through the years, and did for short periods of time, he had always gone back to it.

This time was different. When we cancelled the lawn service, he said, "Look at it this way—it's a win-win. We'll save money and I'll get the exercise I need by mowing the lawn. I haven't felt well for the past six months or so, and know I really have to quit smoking this time."

That day I hadn't noticed Rob had trouble mowing the lawn, because I was busy getting ready for my work week ahead. We had a very nice family dinner, then relaxed watching television.

About eleven o'clock Rob and I decided to go to bed. It had been a long day and we were tired.

I remember feeling really strange, like bugs were crawling all over my body. I have no idea what caused that sensation, or the strange compulsion to take pictures earlier in the day, but those weird feelings freaked me out. I finally said, "I'm going to take a Benadryl. It's the only way I'll be able to fall asleep tonight."

At that point I didn't know how frequently Rob had been having chest pains. I learned later Dr. Mercurio told him it was just anxiety every time, so thinking he was overreacting, eventually Rob stopped telling me about his chest pains. One time he did say, "He's told me the same thing so many times, I'm beginning to feel like I'm crazy."

As the months ticked by, he'd learned to live with the pains and numbness in his left arm because it always went away. And apparently his doctor thought it was all in his head.

But that night was very different. I didn't learn until later that he had awakened about two in the morning with severe chest pains and spent two hours downstairs waiting for them to pass. I was in deep sleep after taking the Benadryl.

Just before four in the morning the pains got worse and I heard him shuffling around the foot of the bed.

Still half-asleep, I said, "What are you doing?"

His voice sounded strange. "I don't feel good. I'm looking for some clothes to go to the hospital. Go back to sleep."

Fully awake now, I sat up in bed. "Hospital? Are you having those chest pains again?"

He didn't answer me right away, then said, "Never mind. I'll wait and go later."

There was no way that was going to happen. "No," I said, springing out of bed. "I'll take you." I tried to keep the panic out of my voice.

One thing I knew for certain. Rob would never go to the emergency room unless he felt like he was dying. I was on instant alert. Something was radically wrong. He always complained that if you weren't admitted the co-payment was five hundred dollars. He didn't even like paying the fifty dollar co-payment for the cardiologist to tell him nothing was wrong. I grabbed a sweatshirt and ran downstairs.

Casey must have heard me and called out, "What's going on?"

I yelled upstairs, "Daddy doesn't feel good. I'm going to take him to the hospital." Rob was walking out the door already as though he was possessed. No phone, wallet or keys—nothing.

Casey had parked behind me in the driveway, but I was operating on automatic pilot. *No time to move the cars. Truck. We'll take his truck.* Everything became surreal. My heart and mind raced. There was no question in my mind that this was a life or death situation.

Rob's truck was parked in the street and by the time I got outside, he was already sitting in the passenger seat.

"What's the fastest way to get to the hospital?" *Why am I*

asking? I know the way. My voice was as calm as I could keep it, but my mind wouldn't stop racing. I couldn't concentrate.

Rob repeated the directions in a low, calm voice and I drove as fast as I could.

We didn't have conversation on the way to the hospital. He was in pain and I was driving like an Indy 500 racecar driver. In hindsight I wish I would have asked him more questions about what was going on. He wasn't clutching his chest, which is always the sign that it's really bad in movies, but I knew instinctively it was really bad. I ran all of the lights and screeched to a stop in front of the emergency room.

"Can you walk in by yourself while I park the truck?"

His voice sounded weak, but he managed to say, "Yeah."

I watched him enter the emergency room door before I parked the truck and ran inside.

The security officer at the desk said, "They've just taken him in for treatment. You can follow." The tone of his voice scared me.

As the automatic doors opened I could see a nurse ahead of me pushing Rob in a wheelchair, and she seemed to be moving very fast. I hurried to catch up to them.

They put him on a stretcher and began to question him. "Where's the pain, how long has the pain been going on," and other questions about his symptoms. He had a hard time answering the questions and that was when I found out he had been up since two o'clock that morning, when the chest pains began.

I'm usually a very light sleeper, but with the Benadryl I had been out cold. I kept telling myself if I hadn't taken the medication I probably would have heard Rob earlier. And then the question I didn't want to ask myself—what would have happened if I hadn't awakened?

Through the years I've always felt more guilt than most people. That's probably because of everything leading up to and following my father's murder. Months upon months of headlines screaming about how guilty I was.

Fear gripped me. *This is not going to be good at all.*

Chapter 18

ROB

THE NIGHT I DIED

WHEN WE GOT HOME FROM THE DINNER, I remember thinking about coaching my daughter Casey's softball game the coming Tuesday. I'd decided this was probably gonna be my last year of coaching because she was seventeen, and when she started college in the fall she wouldn't be playing travel ball anymore. Although I enjoyed coaching all my girls on the team, it was something I did especially for Casey, and it would have felt weird continuing without her. It may sound funny, but I actually looked at it almost as though I'd be betraying her.

Instead of just going inside, I called to Cheryl, "Hey, it's still light. I could use some exercise. I'm going to mow the lawn. Shouldn't take too long."

I took the mower out of the shed and began mowing in back of the house. We had several episodes of *Grey's Anatomy* on DVR and planned to eat Chinese food and watch a *Grey's Anatomy* marathon together after I finished. We always spent a lot of time together as a family, but that night there seemed to be something pushing me to finish the job quickly so we'd have as much time as possible.

Without pausing, I mowed the front lawn right after I finished the back. I was nearly done when suddenly I couldn't catch my breath and had pains in my chest much more severe than the ones I'd been having for the past six months. It felt so strange, I leaned against my truck parked on the street in front of the house while I waited for it to pass.

It was pretty much like the episode I had a week or two before while I was at work, but I'd seen Dr. Mercurio and after checking me out he assured me it was nothing but anxiety. He'd told me that so many times, like Cheryl said I'd even stopped telling her when I had the pains.

Yeah, maybe there really isn't anything wrong this time, either. No worries. It's gotta be all in my head.

Sure enough, after resting a minute or two I felt okay and finished the lawn, put the mower away, went into the house, and didn't say anything about what had happened. I know, I know— big mistake! I had no idea right then just how big it was going to be.

The Chinese food came and we all enjoyed the meal together while chatting.

"Big week coming up," I said. "Hard to believe it will be the final week of any games for us since our team won't make the playoffs."

"End of my high school softball career, too," Casey answered. "It feels a little weird, Dad."

"Well, Senior Day is Tuesday, and I can't wait," I said.

Cheryl added with a chuckle, "That doesn't surprise me. You never missed a game when Casey played, so I guess it's like the end of a high school career for you, too."

She was right. During Casey's senior year it had been very important to me to be there for her and for the team on the field behind her. I knew how frustrating it was for her if she pitched a great game and the team lost because of errors made behind her.

My daughter and I had all sorts of signs and faces we made at each other so both of us knew what the other was thinking. I taught her the game the way my father taught me.

"Yeah, it's kinda sad that it's all coming to an end. No more sneaking out of my job around three-thirty on Tuesdays to put on my 'coach hat.' We'll still have one last time next Tuesday, though. They know I'm leaving work at three so I won't miss one moment of the Senior Day festivities."

No one ever said anything when I'd left early all of those Tuesdays—one of the perks of being at my job for so many years. They weren't as understanding at Cheryl's job, so she didn't get to go to as many games as I did. I felt it was important for her to be at Casey's Senior Day game from the beginning, so I planned to pick my wife up and make sure she was there.

As Casey's parents, we looked at that evening as our time to thank her for all the great memories she'd given us. After dinner we gathered around the TV for our *Grey's* marathon. Around eleven we all said goodnight and got ready for bed. After I got into bed, I remember having a weird sensation—one that I can't really explain.

I have very little conscious memory of what I said or did afterwards. I have a vague recollection of not feeling good again and leaving my bedroom about two in the morning to go downstairs. I didn't want to bother Cheryl because she had taken a Benadryl, so she was sound asleep.

By all later indications, I should have died on my couch that night, but instead of staying on the couch I went back to my bedroom where, according to Cheryl, I made noise and she woke up.

She later told me when she asked what I was doing, I said, "Shhhh. I'm getting dressed and going to the ER. You go back to sleep."

See, I'd been trying to make myself believe that what my car-

- 113 -

diologist told me was true—the pain I'd felt in my chest over the past several months wasn't really "chest pain", but rather all in my head. But this time it was so bad, I thought, "He's a dick. This might be in my head, but I better make sure."

Cheryl jumped out of bed. "You're not going alone. I'll drive."

If not for her, I very well might not have gone to Brookhaven Hospital that night. I felt so bad by then I wasn't sure I could drive anyway, but the pain had passed and I probably would have waited, figuring I could go in the morning. If I'd done that and gone back downstairs, there is no doubt I would have died right there on the same couch I am sitting on as I write my part of this book. It's kinda surreal sitting here and thinking about that.

I really don't have much memory of leaving my house and going to the hospital, except for what I've been told.

Chapter 19

CHERYL

BETWEEN LIFE AND DEATH

THEY ORDERED A CHEST X-RAY IMMEDIATELY while the nurse asked, "Do you have pain in your neck, or just your chest?"

Rob's voice was strained. "My chest. It's in my chest. A lot of pressure. My left arm is numb."

The x-ray tech came into the room and said, "Can you sit up? I need to put a portable screen behind your back to take the x-ray."

I'd been at the foot of the stretcher giving the registrar the insurance information when all of a sudden Rob made a horrendous sound—a sound I cannot describe to this day, but one I never want to hear again. I still hear it over and over again in my nightmares and relive looking over at him and seeing his arms fly back violently and that the noise coming from him—the scariest sound I have ever heard.

His head was pulled back, his eyes rolled back in his head, his mouth wide open, his body tightly stretched out as far as it could go. *Was it a seizure?*

"Help! Please someone help!" I screamed. The nurse was still in the room and she hit the code blue button. Everybody came flying into his room. Still thinking it was a seizure, I moved out of their way into the hallway. I'd worked in the Emergency Room for almost seven years and I'd seen many seizures, but I kept thinking that usually your body just flops around like a fish out of water. Rob was not doing that. His body was stiff and the sound he was making was not a noise I'd ever heard people with seizures make. The code blue alarm was going off. When I looked in, someone was doing CPR on him.

Why CPR? You definitely don't do CPR on a seizure patient. Oh God. Something is really wrong.

They pulled the curtain shut after squeezing in all the medical staff that could fit into his room. My head was spinning. I paced in the hallway as fast as I could, back and forth, back and forth, the length of his room. The faster I paced the more I prayed!

Every minute or so I peeked in. They were working on him furiously. His head was still off to the side with his eyes rolled back, and as more time went by he began to turn a funny color. His body was floundering now, his limp feet swinging side to side while they were doing the compressions. I tried to stay calm, but they were hitting his chest so hard, I could hear the sound out in the hall.

Thoughts flew through my mind like a speeding train. *What's taking so long? Why isn't he alright by now? Can this seriously be happening? Rob walked in there on his own. He's the strongest man I know. Why is he on that stretcher so lifeless?*

For a while I wasn't in touch with reality. I continued to pace back and forth as fast as I could, waiting for Rob to run through the door to help me. *Where is he? What is taking him so long to come and help me through this!* For all the twenty-seven years we were together he was always the one to save me, to make me feel better, and to help me through everything. He had always been there. Good, bad, or indifferent, he was always there!

The frantic words repeated over and over in my mind. Where is he! Where is he!

An inner voice brought me back to the present. *He's not coming this time, Cheryl. He's the one on the stretcher!*

I felt so lost. *What if he doesn't make it?*

I was pacing back and forth frantically when this jackass of a lady came out of the room next to Rob's. "Where is everyone?" she shouted. Her voice got louder and higher pitched. "You need to come right now. My daughter has to go to the bathroom. What kind of a place is this, anyway?"

That sent me over the edge. "Really, lady, really?" I shouted at her. "I'm sorry your daughter needs to use the bathroom, but you see everyone is busy in there trying to save my husband's life."

She just looked at me and calmed down. "I'm sorry. I didn't know."

At that point they had someone come over to stay with me. I'm not sure if the person was a nurse, but obviously the staff didn't want me to be alone. So there we were. This person kept pacing back and forth with me.

Finally she said, "Maybe you should sit." I remember thinking maybe she couldn't keep up with me, maybe she was tired of feeling like she was running a marathon.

She tried to hold my arm to help me walk. I yanked my arm away and shouted, "Just let go. Stop touching me."

"But I'm supposed to make sure you don't fall or pass out."

I'm not a person who can stand to be touched! Visions of all the times I was touched by my father flashed through my mind. Then the visions changed into being touched by the guards as they searched me when I was in jail.

Maybe if I kept walking I could finally get off this merry go round. *Why can't anyone understand I just need to walk? If she doesn't let go and stop touching me, she's gonna be the one to fall or pass out.* I finally said to her, "What should I do?"

"You need to call your family."

Family? Ever since I was sixteen years old I have always been able to call Rob. Not thinking at the moment she probably meant my daughters and anyone else close, I said, "My family is in that room! And, I can't call him."

Instead of being my salvation, my husband, the one person in my life I could always depend upon to make things okay, was fighting for his life and I was terrified.

I stood there in that emergency room with my phone in my hand and decided she was right. It was probably time to call our girls—the hardest phone call I ever had to make.

Chapter 20

CHERYL

MY WORST FEAR CAME TRUE

I STOOD THERE SHAKING, THE PHONE gripped tightly in my hand. In the movies, they tell you to call the family when the end is near. But, how could that be? I couldn't imagine life without Rob.

My mind raced. *How do I get my girls here without making them too upset to drive?* Even though Casey was awake when we left, I decided it would be better to call Sam. I knew Casey had gotten Sam up to tell her we went to the hospital because Sam had texted "Is Daddy okay?"

When that text came in, we were just in the process of giving all the information, so I'd answered "yes" before all hell broke loose.

I said in as calm a voice as I could manage, "Sam, you girls need to come to the hospital as fast as you can, but please drive safely."

"Okay, Mom." She hung up and I was grateful I didn't have to say any more over the phone.

Then I called Rob's sister Liz on her cell instead of the house phone. She answered right away.

By that time, the adrenaline that keeps you going in an

- 119 -

emergency was wearing off. I felt so alone and scared, I was barely able to hold myself together.

"Liz?" I said in a cracking voice that probably didn't sound like me at all.

"Who is this?"

Holding back the sobs, I said, "It's Cheryl. You need to come to Brookhaven Hospital. Now!"

She must have heard the fear in my voice because she said "Okay, I'll be right there," and hung up—no questions.

I started pacing again, and remember thinking, Wow, it's been such a long time. In reality it had been about thirty minutes.

I always felt my mother had sent Rob to help and protect me for the rest of my life—something she couldn't do. So I began to pray to her. "Please, Mom, you have to help me. You sent Rob to me when you died. I still need him with me! I can't go through this life without him."

I prayed to Rob's grandfather Carl, whom we both loved, adored, and looked up to. Before his grandfather died, Rob and I felt so lucky to be able to spend a lot of time with him. I never really knew a man like him before. He was an awesome father and husband, and an even better grandfather.

I even prayed to Rob's baby brother Christopher, who died at birth. He always talked about Baby Christopher being his angel, so I knew I had to pray to him.

I reached back to the time after my trial and prayed to our neighbor, my mother's best friend Birdie, whose real name is Alberta. They lived next door while I was growing up and we were all like family. She was an important mother figure in my life.

"Birdie," I said as I paced in the corridor outside Rob's room, "I really need your help. You know I've never asked anybody for help and always tried to be strong and work things out myself. But, Birdie, this time I think it's out of my hands. Please help me."

After praying to Birdie, my thoughts strayed to what it was like so many years ago. My mom had grown up with Birdie's husband, Big Mike. Their kids, Michael and AnnMarie, are very close to me, my younger sister JoAnn and older brother Jimmy to this day. This feeling of family has continued through the generations. Our kids and their kids, Amanda and Mikey, are as close as we are with AnnMarie and James and we all spend a lot of time together.

After my mom died, Birdie took care of us kids as though she was our mother. I found out later that she promised my mother she would always take good care of her children once she was gone, and Birdie kept her promise.

She had a lot of battles with cancer through the years, but always managed to surprise us with her strength, courage, and willpower. Then the time came when she was losing the battle.

She said, "I'm sorry this is happening to me because I won't be able to keep the promise I made to your mother."

With a lump in my throat, I said, "You got me through the hardest time in my life. Don't say you didn't keep your promise. It's okay for you to rest now. It's time for you to be with my mother.

She died a few hours after that conversation. If anyone knew how much Rob and I had been through together and how much we loved each other, it was Birdie.

I hesitated a moment, and then as a last resort sucked in a deep breath and decided I needed to pray to my father. No matter how bad things have gotten for me, and no matter how low I've felt, I have never prayed to him before—never even tried to acknowledge him in my thoughts. I still hold deep resentment after all these years, and swore I would never ask him for anything. But now was the time to call in everyone to help. Especially him.

I prayed, "Dad, I need your help. I never asked you for

anything. You owe me. You owe me big! If you're sorry, truly sorry for what you did to me, then make it up to me and help Rob. You need to do this for me. You need to make Rob okay!"

While all this was running through my head a mile a minute, I kept peeking in on Rob's room and clutching my phone. The sound of it ringing broke through my thoughts and prayers.

"Mom, it's Sam. I can't find the emergency room entrance."

What do I do now? Do I leave the outside of Rob's room to find them or do I stay and let them try to find it by themselves?

If Rob dies, I want him to have family by his side, not just strangers. What would he want me to do?

In my heart I knew he would have wanted me to meet them. As I left to find the girls, the lady who had been pacing with me kept pulling my arm and trying to keep up.

I found the girls in the parking lot, all disheveled and still in their pajamas. Both of them cried at the same time, "We left right after you called. What's wrong?"

By that time I was beyond being able to answer them. The lady, still trying to keep up with me, led us back into the hospital. She pointed to the grieving room for families and said to the girls, "Stay in this room. We're going to check on your father and we'll let you know what's going on."

I started walking back to Rob's room with the lady, but when I turned and looked behind me, the girls were following us. I think for the first time in their lives, I was glad they didn't listen.

Another nurse came up to us and said, "The doctor needs to see you."

I asked, "Why?"

She answered, "Please, just come with me."

Without thinking about it, I said, "If he's dead just tell me now." This couldn't possibly be real. I was going to wake up soon. At least that's what I told myself.

She replied, "He's not, but you need to come quickly."

I said to our girls, "Come on, please come with me." At that point, I wasn't sure I could make it myself.

We walked down the hall to Rob's room with me in the middle and my girls on each side of me. We were holding each other up. The doctor was standing outside Rob's door, looking very somber.

My heart stopped. Everything was very fuzzy and seemed like it was in slow motion.

I will never forget the doctor's voice when he said, "There was nothing more we could do for your husband. I'm very sorry."

Easter 1980 - first of many holidays spent in hospital with mom.

Birdie and Big Mike - couldn't of made it without you.

June 1985 - became boyfriend and girlfriend.

With my best friend Cocoa whom I couldn't save.

These 2 amazing people made Rob the person he is today.

My best friend Rocky boy.

INCEST, MURDER AND A MIRACLE

One of the best days of my life.

My brother, my super hero, always by my side.

I will always protect you JoAnn and have your back.

My mother-in-law the woman who never gave up on me.

CHERYL AND ROBERT CUCCIO WRITTEN WITH MORGAN ST. JAMES

This Is what death looks like.

October 2016 Still going strong.

July 2016 - So blessed our family is all together, even Brody.

The loves of my life.

Chapter 21

CHERYL

FIGHTING FOR ROB'S LIFE

I COULD STILL HEAR THEM POUNDING on Rob's chest, and thought maybe I hadn't heard him right. *Why would they still be doing CPR if Rob was dead?* I gave the doctor a questioning look.

His next words chilled me to the core. "Mrs. Cuccio, I'm so sorry. We really tried, but we couldn't get his heart started. He's been without a pulse for more than thirty minutes now."

By that time, my heart was pounding so hard it felt as though it would explode if I even took a small breath. My daughters were next to me and I was speaking up for them as well as myself. I couldn't bear the thought of giving up on my husband—their father.

The sounds I heard in the background seemed to move very fast, while everything else felt as though it was in slow motion. Loud noises from all the commotion going on spilled into the hallway as the medical staff worked on Rob. I fought to remain standing and needed to catch my breath. It felt like I had been punched in my stomach so hard, I would vomit if I spoke. My feelings intensified. The lights in the hallway seemed so bright it hurt my eyes just to keep them open.

As a child I was taught children should be seen but not heard when in the company of adults, and to respect my elders. Whether the adult was right or wrong, I was never allowed to speak up for myself. The knowledge that my opinion didn't matter had been drummed into me to such a degree that I'd lived in fear of confrontation my entire life.

Even though I'd worked on building my confidence through the years, I still was never able to build it to the point where I could challenge the opinion of an authority figure. And, believe me, the doctor was an authority figure. But when he said nothing more could be done for my husband, something inside me crashed through the fear. Everything in me said I had to challenge authority and not back down. I had to do everything possible to try to save my husband.

This new feeling of empowerment went against everything in my soul, everything I'd been brainwashed to believe, but this wasn't a dress rehearsal. If I didn't speak up and demand that they keep trying, Rob would be lost to me forever. I reached down to my very core, summoning every bit of strength and confidence as possible. When I implored the doctor to keep trying in a very firm voice, my expectation that he would came through loud and clear.

Caught somewhere between pleading and demanding, I wasn't going to give up. "Can't you just cut him open and pump his heart with your hands?" I demanded.

There was pain in the doctor's eyes when he said, "No, I'm so sorry, we don't do that at this hospital."

Really. I thought all hospitals are supposed to do everything and anything to save a patient's life.

Without giving an inch, I said out loud, "Well, you need to keep trying." I pointed to my daughters, who were as much in shock as I was. "These are his children. My husband is only forty-four years old." My voice rose. "Please! You have to keep trying. I know he wouldn't leave us."

Thank God the ER wasn't busy that day, or he might not have looked at me and said, "Okay. We'll try for another ten minutes, but please understand—that will be all. Then you'll have to let him go." At that point, I didn't know Rob had been pronounced dead already.

Tears filled my eyes. "Okay. Thank you."

It was an amazing moment for me because I realized I was speaking up for more than my husband's life. I was speaking up for the scared little girl who was abused most of her childhood and for the adult I had grown into. Drawing upon the strength I learned from my husband, I silently thanked him for teaching me that I was a strong confident woman whose opinion *does* matter.

Our girls followed the doctor into Rob's room to see their dad for what might be the last time.

Casey and Sam wanted to try to wake him up in those last ten minutes. The air in the corridor grew heavy, the medicinal smell almost gagging me. I felt a little lightheaded and my heart thumped like crazy. Would this be it?

Looking back, when my girls walked into his room they saw a young male in blue scrubs straddling their dad's cold, lifeless, grayish body—a body that didn't even look like their dad any longer.

I heard their scared voices. "Come on, Dad. You can do this! Wake up, Dad—come on, please, you can do this, Dad." They tried to be strong, cheering Rob on as he fought to come back to life while the sounds of all the machines beeped and echoed in our heads. Even with all the medical staff working diligently to save him, this craziness in the room, they tried with all their hearts to get him to wake up. I was so proud of them.

After they came back into the corridor, they watched the digital clock outside his room. About six minutes had passed. We knew we only had four minutes left when Liz came running down the hallway yelling, "What's the matter, what's the matter?"

I couldn't speak. All I could do was point to Rob's room. She pulled the curtain back and screamed, "What the hell happened? What's going on? That should be me in that bed, not my brother. I'm the sick one."

Crying hysterically, she pushed me and began to pound on my chest.

In an effort to calm her down, I said, "Liz, please, I called you because I needed your help for my kids—please."

What the hell do I do now?

I'd no sooner said that than Casey was standing behind her. She picked Liz up by her arms and sat her in the chair. Even though it was me Liz was beating on, Casey said in as calm a voice as she could muster while trying to mask her fear, "Stop screaming, Aunt Liz. You're scaring my dad."

Liz had always been so unruffled. She'd been an RN ever since she graduated college almost twenty-five years before. Always strong and under control, I'd never expected that reaction. But my sister-in-law was truly a wreck and I felt terrible for her.

Looking back, Liz hadn't been prepared to see what she saw. She hadn't asked any questions when I'd urged her to come to the hospital. Although we told her Rob was having chest pain over the past several months and was going to the cardiologist, it didn't prepare any of us for what was happening now.

A noise came from Rob's room. "Oh my God," I thought, "it sounds like clapping." The clock had two minutes remaining, and to our joy and amazement, all of the medical staff in the room were cheering.

What could they be clapping and cheering about? My husband is dying.

I couldn't believe what I heard next when the doctor came into the corridor. "Your husband has a pulse. He is truly a medical miracle. I can't explain it, because there is no way your husband should have a pulse after all this time without one, but he does and now we need to get him to Stony Brook University Hospital as fast as we can."

The doctor said, "A Stony Brook ambulance is in the parking lot and they'll transport him there right away." I later learned that generally a Stony Brook ambulance is not on the grounds, but again, fate was on our side.

Still trying to take in everything that had happened, I said, "Okay."

Liz turned to me and said, "I want to call his cardiologist right now."

By now, everything was a blur to me, and I had to fight to stay alert. I pulled his card from my wallet and gave it to her. As they prepared Rob for transport to Stony Brook, Liz called Dr. Mercurio, the doctor Rob had now been seeing for at least six months, but reached his answering service. It was still so early in the morning, the office wasn't open yet.

In her firm nurse's voice, she said, "You need to get him on the phone *now*. I want to know what the hell is going on and I want to talk to him." It turned out his partner was on call and Dr. Mercurio wasn't available.

When Liz told him what happened, Dr. Mercurio's partner said, "I didn't treat that patient and know nothing of his case."

Liz hung up and called her husband, Scott, to tell him what happened. When he got to the hospital, he said, "We'll pick Mom up and tell her what's happened to Rob. Go ahead to Stony Brook and we'll meet you there."

In the meantime, the nurse said, "You can go with your husband in the ambulance," which was great news.

Our girls were still wearing their pajamas, and I told them, "I'm going to ride in the ambulance with Dad, and you should go home, get dressed, and meet us at Stony Brook." Thinking back,

- 131 -

what a dumbass I was. Casey had just gotten her license and she would have to drive Rob's big Dodge Ram truck all by herself while Sam drove home in her own car. After everything those kids had endured, all the emotions they just went though and everything they saw, how could I have felt they would be safe driving around town by themselves?

Obviously I wasn't thinking straight by that time, because under normal circumstances I would never have done that. But, he was alive now and in my mind everything was going to be okay, so there was just one more thing that had to be done.

After everybody left, I sat there outside Rob's room watching them begin to put all the portable equipment on him so they could transport him to Stony Brook Hospital. With the main crisis over, I was able to think about who else I needed to call.

Operating in a daze, first I called North Shore Hematology/ Oncology, where Rob worked. Sam was also working there while she was home from college. It was a rough call, but I managed to tell their boss neither of them would be into work that day.

I'd totally forgotten it was my forty-third birthday until I noticed a message from my boss saying "Happy Birthday." So I texted, "Can I call you?" When I called her, I told her what had happened.

Chapter 22

CHERYL

I HAD TO STAY STRONG

WHILE I SAT THERE WATCHING THEM pack Rob up for the trip to Stony Brook, I recognized one of the ambulance people from the hospital where I worked and said, "Just so you know, I'm going with you."

He looked straight at me with pity written all over his face. "I'm sorry. We can't let you do that."

At first I thought maybe I heard wrong. During all the years I worked in the ER, I saw family members go to Stony Brook with their family in the transport ambulance, so I knew it's allowed. Generally it's only one family member, but they do let at least one go.

So I tried one more time. "This is my husband and I *am* going."

Again he said, "No. I'm sorry. You can't go."

This didn't make sense. "How come? I should be able to."

He answered, "It would be too dangerous. We'll be driving very fast and running red lights, because we need to get him there as fast as possible."

I still didn't accept that. "Don't you think if I don't go with you it will be just as dangerous for me? I'll be right behind you running red lights as well."

When he shrugged and said, "I'm sorry, you just can't go with us," I walked away. At that point I didn't have enough energy left to fight with anyone.

Now what the hell am I going to do? Everyone left and I don't have a car here.

I didn't want to make our girls drive back to get me, but they had driven both of our cars home. Finally I called Sam and asked her to come back to Brookhaven and pick me up. Actually, it worked out better because the girls wouldn't have to drive all the way to Stony Brook Hospital alone.

Rob still wasn't ready, so I just sat there. It seemed like it took forever to get him prepared, but I knew they were going as fast as they could. The longer I waited, the more worried I became.

The girls returned to Brookhaven and sat with me, watching as the medical staff got their dad ready for transport. Sam tried for a light moment in a sea of hurt. She said with a weak smile, "Dad will do anything to get out of buying you a present for your birthday, huh?"

We all just chuckled a little, and then Casey added a little more black humor. "He *would* die on your birthday, just so you'll think of him every year and not be able to celebrate without him."

Well, these days Rob has two birthdays—September 22, 1967, the day his mother gave birth to him, and May 14, 2012, the day he died for forty-three minutes and came back to us. Now we celebrate my birthday and his birthday on the same day every year.

Time continued to drag on, and I said to the girls, "I would like to use the bathroom before we go."

They said, "Okay, we'll go with you."

I barely made it to the bathroom. I threw my guts up for at

least three minutes. It felt so good to do that. My insides had been turned upside down from the time we sped to the hospital in a race against death, and I could finally let it out. I felt much better, washed up, and went back outside.

We saw the young guy who had been performing CPR on Rob, covered in sweat and looking exhausted. I walked over to him, shook his hand, and said, "Thank you so much for all your hard work. I'll never forget you."

"No problem. I hope he's okay."

Rob was finally ready, so we watched them put him in the ambulance, then got in Sam's car. I drove, and I followed the ambulance the best I could. It was never out of my sight, as the siren cleared traffic. I don't know to this day how I was able to drive, knowing how unstable my husband—my best friend—was as he fought for his life in that ambulance without me.

He's with strangers. They don't know anything about him kept running through my head. I felt myself getting upset, but had to be strong for our girls. I needed to hear a friendly voice telling me everything would be alright. That's when I decided to call my brother in Tennessee to tell him what happened, because that's what Jimmy does. He makes you believe everything will work out.

Instead, after I told him what had happened, I heard my brother—one of the strongest people I know—losing it over the phone. Now I'd said it out loud and felt even worse because I'd upset him so much. Not only that, but it forced me to recognize the reality of what happened.

Jimmy said he would drop everything and rush to New York to be with us. I calmed down a little, knowing Jimmy would be the rock I needed to keep from falling apart while Rob fought for his life.

Sometimes I think if you don't say things out loud they don't seem real. I got through so much of my young life that way. But when you hear yourself say something out loud, you are admit-

- 135 -

ting to yourself that it does exist. Maybe what kept me strong throughout this horrible ordeal was not admitting to myself what was happening to our family.

No matter how quickly he had reacted, it still took time to get from Tennessee to New York. Knowing that Rob had already died once, I'm sure Jimmy hoped and prayed he would get there in time if Rob was going to die again.

Inner terror is a feeling I know too well and I really related to it. When my mother's condition became critical, my father picked me up at school early so many times I can't even count them. Each time we would rush to the hospital in the city hoping to make it there before she died.

The tables had turned. I had to face the fact that I needed to be the strong one until Jimmy arrived. The two men who have always helped me get through every trauma in my life needed me to be stronger than ever without their help.

I would be the person they needed me to be. This time I was in control.

Chapter 23

CHERYL

MY BROTHER JIMMY

FOR A WHILE AFTER MY FATHER WAS murdered, the more I confronted things and was able to talk about what had happened, the more I began to feel better little by little. Because of what I did, maybe you don't see me as also being a victim of my father's murder, but I was, and it took a while, and I mean *a while*, for my physical and mental systems to settle down. I hated my father, was mad at my mother, and didn't understand my brother. Right after it happened, the relationship between Jimmy and me was a little strained.

While I lived next door at the Kosser's house awaiting my hearing, Jimmy moved back into our house. So we lived right next to each other. Jimmy had a lot of parties, with his friends trooping in and out of our family's house night and day. There was drinking and drugs, and I'd see them passed out all over. Our mother's things were getting broken, some stuff was stolen from the house, and Jimmy just didn't seem to care.

It was as though in his mind he was getting back at our father and his rigid rules by not doing what my father would have wanted done. Thinking about it, I'd get so angry at him. *How could he disrespect our house and all the things our mother loved?*

I realize now he was going through a really rough time, too. I guess he did a lot of drinking and drugs to get through the pain. He was just nineteen and with both of his parents dead, found himself in charge of the entire estate of someone he despised. It was a big responsibility.

He had lost so much during the two years leading up to the murder, and to top it off found out his sister had hired someone to kill his father, who had been sexually abusing her for six years. Maybe if I wasn't so afraid of becoming dependent on drugs and alcohol, I would have responded the same way he did. But, I'd been helpless for so long, I was afraid of not being in control. Helpless was a feeling I never wanted again.

By the February after our father was shot and killed in our driveway, Jimmy and I became very close again. He was extremely protective of me and blamed himself for my not being able to go to him and tell him the truth about the incest and abuse our father constantly subjected me to. When it first came out in the open, he never doubted that any of it was true, but did say, "Why didn't you tell me what was happening? I would have ended it myself."

Actually, I'd sort of tried one time when I hinted at it, but that's all it was—a hint about doing away with our father. In reality, I was afraid if he really knew what was going on he definitely would have done something to end it himself.

I never expected Sean would really murder my father, but I'm glad it wasn't Jimmy because he would have gone to jail for a really long time. When he finally found out the reality of my sordid existence, he was so hurt he said, "I want to go to the cemetery and dig him up. I'd like to put his body in the dump where it belongs. I don't want that asshole buried next to our mother."

I was able to talk Jimmy out of doing that by saying, "Mommy

INCEST, MURDER AND A MIRACLE

is in heaven and he is not, so just leave it alone and let Mommy rest in peace." But we did agree that his name would never be put on her tombstone.

Listening to the testimony drone on in the courtroom, I imagined what horrible feelings Jimmy must have had when I called on the way to Stony Brook Hospital to tell him Rob, his best friend, had died and was brought back to life in very critical condition. It was hard to control the overwhelming feelings I had toward Dr. Mercurio at that moment.

◆ ◆ ◆

I put my memories aside for a few minutes so I could listen as testimony in our malpractice suit continued, but I couldn't concentrate.

The thought of what my life would be like now if I'd said okay when the doctor told me there was nothing else they could do for Rob haunted me. It's hard enough to handle things like this under normal circumstances, but because I deal with PTSD on a daily basis caused by all of the abuse in my early life, everything becomes magnified under pressure.

I pictured all the times Rob never gave up on me, how he helped and supported me through a lot of tough times. Because of the horrors that made up my life when my father was alive, the murder, the time spent in jail, I have a lot of issues that continued through the years. I have never told anyone else about them except Rob. He knows how I've struggled with the nightmares, the moodiness, trust issues, anxiety, self-esteem, the issues I have with sex—I could go on and on.

He saved my life so many times. Every time I wanted to give up and not get out of bed because I felt like I was just damaged goods, he and my daughters got me through the day. On that awful day three years before, because I knew if I wasn't as strong as possible I would have lost him forever, I was able to summon

- 139 -

everything in me to save his life.

Sometimes when I think about everything that happened, I wonder if I couldn't give up on Rob because I was being selfish for me and our girls. To this day I can't explain the determination that drove me, but I know for sure I wasn't ready for him to leave us.

Thoughts and images swirled in my mind. The courtroom suddenly felt stuffy and I imagined the walls were closing in on me. One thought repeated over and over in my mind: *I want justice for what Rob went through. This doctor didn't see what was really happening to him.*

Then I wondered how many people die after thirty minutes or less because they don't have family refusing to give up on them. Maybe the person with them can't handle the situation or think to ask for more time. Maybe nobody close to them is there fighting for their life. What about the doctors who won't give another try? I couldn't shut those thoughts off.

My heart pounded like a wild drum solo as I imagined all those people who died but might have been medical miracles like Rob if only they had someone fighting for them—someone asking for ten more minutes. It doesn't mean they would have survived, but at least they would have had that last chance.

I still think about that often, and one day when our lives are a little calmer, I would like to try to make a difference by having as many people as possible know our story through this book and also give motivational talks. I have a mission to help abused children, which is part of the reason I am writing about the horrors of my early life. I truly believe it was everything I went through that gave me the strength and determination to fight so hard for Rob.

When our attorney, Russell Corker, questioned Dr. Mercurio, I really wanted to hear every bit of his testimony, but my mind kept jumping back to memories of that awful day. However, when it sounded like something important was being covered, I did snap back to attention. Unfortunately that didn't happen soon enough, and I realized I'd missed some of his testimony.

The following is taken from court transcripts:

Russell said, "When you told Rob Cuccio that you thought his problem was probably related to food, did you tell him that stress echoes had a percentage of false negatives? Any discussions with him about that?"

Dr. Mercurio's attorney objected, and the judge asked which stress echo test was being referred to.

Russell answered, "Going back to January."

The judge asked, "So, are you asking him the question on April 24th that goes back to January? Is that your question?"

I'd looked over at Rob at that point, then glared at Dr. Mercurio. *Now he's going to get it*, I thought.

Russell redefined his question. "Let me be inclusive. At either one of the visits, Doctor, did you ever advise Mr. Cuccio that passing a stress test doesn't guarantee you don' t have significant coronary artery disease? Any discussions along those lines?"

Dr. Mercurio's attorney objected again and the judge overruled him again, but said, "I mean, we've had discussion here about his memory being mostly from his records, unless he has some independent recollection of the answer to your question." Then he addressed Dr. Mercurio. "So answer it the best you can."

He appeared quite confident about his answer. He said, "Typically, I wouldn't tell a patient about the false negative of a test because I don' t want them to be an emotional wreck. So if they have a normal stress test, I try to reassure them by saying 'you're doing fine'."

I felt my face flush in anger. *Yeah, asshole, he was doing just fine, wasn't he? He could barely make it off the treadmill. Maybe if you'd just mentioned that bit about the possibility of the test being wrong he wouldn't have trusted what you told him and known he was having a heart attack.*

Our attorney posed one more question. "And, Doctor, just a last question. April 24, 2012, under your diagnosis you do not list the cause of his chest pain as anything to do with the food; correct?"

It was hard to listen to this testimony because the doctor managed to sidestep every pertinent question with "I don't remember," or something along those lines. Could it be that Rob's stress test had been questionable, but this doctor told him he was fine? When he couldn't catch his breath, this jerk told Rob not to worry, and now he sat there acting so innocent and professional when so much of his testimony confirmed a bad diagnosis.

What must the jury be thinking?

Chapter 24

ROB

JIMMY AND I ARE CLOSER THAN BROTHERS

SOMETIMES CIRCUMSTANCES CREATE relationships that might not have happened otherwise. In our case, Jimmy and I were drawn together by what had happened to someone we loved dearly. There is nothing I wouldn't do for him and I know he feels the same. He certainly reinforced that the day I died when Cheryl called him and he dropped everything. By the next day he was there for our family. Although Cheryl and Jimmy are very close, over the years the two of us became closer than blood brothers.

He still busts my balls, claiming I owe him a few lawn mowings because he did that for me while I was in a coma. That wasn't all he did. Jimmy took care of our house as if it were his own, and for that I can never repay him. I know he doesn't want anything from me, but he knows all he has to do is call and I will be there for him or his wife, Maureen. I really appreciated how completely Jimmy supported his sister throughout her parole and hearing, too, and I think he appreciated me as well.

Looking back at the big picture of everything that happened in our lives, we are able to laugh about all the trouble we got into together now, but I know I couldn't have gotten through the ordeal of Cheryl being in jail and me being on probation without him.

When I first began to see Cheryl, we kinda had a vague knowledge of each other. Jimmy and I had played against each other in little league for a few seasons. When I was a junior and he was a senior, we had a psychology class together.

I remember the first time I went to Cheryl's house for dinner as her boyfriend. I was a tough guy, or at least thought of myself that way, and I really didn't care what Jimmy thought of me now that I was his sister's boyfriend. In fact, I didn't really care what anyone thought. Friends told me she was too young—Cheryl was a sophomore and I was a senior—but I could care less.

So, Jimmy and I never really had much interaction until the shit hit the fan after the murder and our lives turned into the stuff movies are made of. At the beginning Jimmy and I actually kinda hated each other. During the year we were awaiting the hearing, Jimmy lived in the Pierson house and Cheryl lived with her neighbors Birdie and Big Mike. The houses shared one lawn, and I saw how Jimmy was trashing "her" house. Not only that, but I couldn't stand the way he tried to keep his sister and me apart.

Jimmy was a drummer in a rock and roll band in the mid-eighties. With the house to himself, he had set up a studio in the living room. Other "rock stars" were there constantly, and while they jammed with no regard for the house and all the possessions in it, everything was getting ruined.

Do I blame Jimmy? No, because his life had turned into something he didn't ask for. We were all kids with no one telling us how we should be acting. Was he irresponsible? I'd have to say, "Yes, he was."

Jimmy crashed three or four of the cars that his father owned, and then took Cheryl's. That pissed Cheryl off, and me as well. Words were exchanged and a feud was on. We never threw down, which was the way I solved most of my problems before I "grew up", but maybe that was the same force that has kept Cheryl and me so close.

Jimmy and I literally hated each other that whole year. Then I guess we came to realize we were both in a whole lot of shit, the same shit, only a little different. A bond began to grow because while people were either for us or against us, we were on the same side and wanted the same outcome.

By the time we came to this realization, the house had been sold and Jimmy had a new apartment. He invited Cheryl and me over for a dinner of homemade tacos, we had some good conversation, and finally smoked the peace pipe. I think we agreed neither of us was going anywhere and we were both in it to the end. I even helped him put down carpet tiles after he lit his cymbal on fire. When he hit it, the cymbal fell and almost set the apartment on fire. Fortunately it was put out before becoming a real disaster, but the carpet got the worst of it, so we had to pull it up and lay the tiles.

After Cheryl was sentenced and sent to jail my relationship with Jimmy grew stronger. We were together every day. At one point my parents were giving me a hard time after I got home from partying, and in a fit of defiance I moved out of my house and drove over to his apartment in Patchogue.

He greeted me at the door, somewhat surprised at my unexpected visit. I didn't take the time for a fancy buildup, and just said, "Hey, I had a fight with my parents and walked out." He gave me a look.

"Okay," I admitted, "what I actually shouted at them was, 'I'm moving out' and left. Can I crash here?"

Without a bit of hesitation he said, "Of course, but you'll have to leave when Cheryl gets out of jail."

Even though I said okay, I think both of us knew that wasn't going to happen.

From that point on we were inseparable. We went to see

Cheryl every day while she was in jail, knowing our visits were the only thing that kept her going. Besides, we wanted to make sure she was safe. She had been through so much, and this jail experience was one more thing that could either make or break her. As I found out much later, it was also one of the things that gave her extreme inner strength when she really needed it.

Then came the day when I couldn't go to the jail with Jimmy because I was in the hospital after hurting my back skitching. When Jimmy got there, she looked at him expectantly. "Where's Rob?"

After a little hemming and hawing, Jimmy finally said, "Um, don't worry. He hurt his back, but he'll be okay. Nothing serious, but they wanted to keep him in the hospital.

Jimmy really didn't want to tell her it happened because I was skitching, but she got it out of him. If you don't know what skitching is, it's something we do here in the Northeast when the roads are icy. You put on shoes with no treads and hold onto the bumper of a car while it pulls you around. Dumb, I know, but we were still young and didn't always relate to possible conse-quences. So, we were doing it on the block where we lived.

I had already gone once and my arms were a little tired, but I wanted to go again. Jimmy was driving over fifty miles an hour—no shit—fifty. Our other friend Craig was looking at me through the back window, then letting Jimmy know how I was doing. Well, I was trying to signal Craig to tell Jimmy to slow down, but he misread me and told him to speed up. By this time my arms felt like rubber and I let go. So there I was free skitching at fifty miles an hour which would have been great if the road was straight, but with my luck we were approaching a curve in the road.

With no way to turn, I was headed straight toward a fence. At that moment I realized I was going to get hurt. I hit the curb, kinda flipped, and hit the fence with my back, then bounced into the middle of the street. I couldn't breathe and my back hurt real bad. The guys pulled up, laughing until they saw I was really hurt.

"Just take me inside the house," I said while gritting my teeth against the pain. The cold and ice made the pain even worse.

"No way," Jimmy said. "I'm calling an ambulance."

They always send a cop when you call an ambulance, so I didn't want Jimmy to make that call. Cheryl, Jimmy, and I hadn't had great experiences with the cops up until then. All I needed was another episode with a cop—I mean she was in jail and I was on probation. As fate would have it, the officer arrived first. He took one look at the situation, scowled, and said, "Who's the brain surgeon that was driving?

Our buddy Craig said, "Um, it was me." Well, he had to say that because Jimmy didn't have a license and would have gone to jail if he said he was driving. One Pierson sibling in jail was enough.

The cop lambasted Craig and said, "Move the car IMMEDI-ATELY!" Now it was like a slapstick comedy routine. Craig didn't know how to drive a stick shift, and stalled the car three times before he was able to move it. As hard as we tried, Jimmy and I couldn't hold back our laughter.

Looking even sterner, the cop said, "And you clowns want me to believe he was driving?" Fortunately, the ambulance came and transported me to Brookhaven Hospital, the same hospital where I was pronounced dead so many years later.

They performed all kinds of tests, then discharged me later that night. The next day I wasn't able to go see Cheryl, and boy was she pissed. Not because I didn't go to see her, but because we were so stupid and I could have really gotten hurt. Although I didn't want to admit it, I knew she was right.

When Cheryl got out of jail and moved in with Jimmy in Patchogue, I never left. He never brought it up to me again, either. We all knew I wasn't going anywhere. I think he saw the love Cheryl and I had when we got engaged the day she got out of jail.

- 147 -

Soon after that Jimmy moved to California to pursue his music career and Cheryl and I took over the apartment and all the bills.

Jimmy is the person I am closest to besides my wife. We talk once or twice a week and he is the go-to person for me.

When Cheryl called him, it was no surprise that he flew to New York to be by my bedside and support his sister. I wouldn't hesitate to do the same for him.

Chapter 25

CHERYL

AT STONY BROOK HOSPITAL

THE SMELL OF A HOSPITAL ALWAYS turns my stomach. I have such bad memories dating back to when my mother was there, and how she never came out. It took me a long time to overcome the way that smell made me feel.

We had followed the ambulance to Stony Brook Hospital and went to the valet parking for the Emergency Room entrance, then ran into the waiting room outside the cardiac unit. As we ran in, we saw my mother in-law, Liz, and my brother in-law, Scott, already standing there.

We hugged them all and I asked my mother in-law, "Are you okay?"

She answered, "Yes, and you?"

I don't recall being able to answer her, but if I did, I'm sure my answer was "no."

We were led to this room I can only remember as being really white and very cold. I'm sure I was operating on automatic pilot by then, was sick to my stomach, and felt like I was in some weird nightmare.

After I'd gotten my job at the hospital, I always had such a sick feeling in my stomach from the time I got to work until I left for the day. I spent almost seven years trying not to let the hospital smells bother me and thought I had overcome it.

Until I walked into Rob's room.

He was hooked up to so many machines, I could hardly get to his bedside. Wherever he had a hole in his body there was some kind of tube coming out of it. The non-stop beeping noises from all the equipment resounded in my head. I remembered as a kid going to the hospital to visit my mom when she was on dialysis and there were a lot of tubes all around her, but nothing ever prepared me for this. One of the first things that struck me was that he didn't even look like himself. I was worried for our girls, but I wasn't going to complain.

An older man wearing a white lab coat came in. He spoke with a very thick accent and it was hard for me to understand him. What I did hear and understand was, "Your husband is in very critical condition. You were not allowed to be in the ambulance during the transport to the hospital because they didn't think he would make it. But he did. We had a miracle when he got his pulse back and then it was a second miracle that he made it through the transport. Now we need a third miracle. He has about a ten percent chance of coming out of the necessary surgery alive."

I took that as good news because it was more than the doctor at Brookhaven Hospital gave us when he pronounced Rob dead and I had begged him for more time. I will never forget the look on that doctor's face when he said, "Just ten more minutes, just ten more minutes." When we are little kids, we beg to stay up for ten more minutes, wish for ten more minutes to finish a test, or know dinner has to stay in the oven for ten more minutes. To me, ten more minutes will forever represent the gift of six hundred seconds that made the difference between my husband living and dying.

The Stony Brook surgeon proceeded to tell us that if he was able to repair Rob's heart, he was still really concerned about his brain, because forty-three minutes without oxygen is an unbelievably long time. Then he said, "Let's just get through this surgery. Then we will figure out what to do next, but I want you to realize that he will never be the normal person he was before this happened and he does only have a ten percent chance of coming through this surgery!"

Ten minutes, ten percent—why are these doctors fixated on the number ten?

The doctor continued, "I'll come out and let you know as soon as we are finished."

I didn't know how many more miracles God would give us. I had lost trust in all doctors yet again, but this time needed to really pray that God would help this surgeon during Rob's operation. I wanted to hug him and beg him, "Please. Do the best work you've ever done."

Rob's life was in his hands. It was scary to know my best friend's life, the father of my children, depended upon how good this man was as a surgeon.

We all walked back into the waiting room and the long wait began. I called Casey's high school varsity softball coach, whom we were very close with, and a few other people. It felt like we were waiting forever, so after two hours or so Liz and I decided we would take a walk to the cath lab where they were doing his surgery. When we got there, we asked, "How much longer?"

Sometimes things can't be explained. What were the odds of Rachel, our next door neighbor who works as a nurse in the cath lab, recognizing our last name on the surgery list and coming to find me? She was a Godsend to me and my family. She came every day to check on us and give her love and support, which I greatly appreciated.

Is it fate? I don't know the answer, but the timeline that day was like a scripted movie. When Rob arrived at Brookhaven, there were no other emergency patients. That meant all the staff could focus their attention and efforts on getting Rob's pulse back. Then the Stony Brook ambulance was already in the parking lot even though ambulances from that hospital were rarely there. It took him to Stony Brook the minute he was ready for transport. He arrived before the scheduled patients and a skilled surgeon was there, ready to work on Rob. Even the timeline in getting Rob to Brookhaven Hospital was like something out of a movie. Think about it. Ten minutes after he arrived he had fully coded. Another of those tens. Had we waited even a few minutes more to leave our house while he literally fought me about going to the hospital, or if I had taken the time to move the cars, it would have been too late. Even if I'd stopped to put on a bra, or been afraid to run the red lights, the outcome wouldn't have been good.

Somewhere in the big plan of things, I believe it was meant to work out.

I felt in my heart things were going to be okay and in my head I just kept praying.

The nurse said to us, "He's coming out of surgery. Go back to the waiting room, and the doctor will be out shortly to talk to you."

I said okay, except I really wanted to say, "Well, did he make it? Can you tell me more?"

But after working in a hospital for many years I knew the nurses cannot give you any information. So we went back to the waiting room and sat in silence until the doctor got us and brought us back to that cold, white room.

He said, "Your husband made it through the surgery. Two main arteries in the back of his heart were ninety percent and one hundred percent clogged. The whole back of his heart was dead and the only reason he was able to get a pulse back was because the front of his heart was still alive."

A very serious look crossed his face. "This never should have happened and your family shouldn't have to be going through this." Then he looked me dead in the eye, almost angrily, and said, "If you need any of my help going after this cardiologist, you just let me know because there is no reason this should have happened. This didn't develop overnight and should have been diagnosed way before it ever got this far."

The words registered, but I didn't care about that right then. I just wanted to know if he was going to be okay.

The doctor said, "I was able to repair his heart and now he has a heart of a twenty-year-old."

Relief flooded through me and I was even able to crack a smile. "Great, that's all Rob will need to hear when he wakes up. Since I turned forty, he's been threatening to trade me in for two twenty-year-olds and I would always say, 'You could never handle them.' Now he probably could!"

The doctor said, "Okay. On a serious note, even though his heart is doing better than when he arrived here, he is no way near out of critical condition. I'm very concerned about his brain. We'll just have to wait to see how bad, if any, the brain suffered from lack of oxygen. That's something we don't know yet."

So, that was where it stood. We would have to wait and see. The doctor gave him a forty percent chance of surviving and although that was still less than half, I was glad the number had improved from the ten percent we were given before the surgery. We went back to the waiting room until Rob was in his room in the cardiac care unit.

◆ ◆ ◆

Dr. Mercurio was on the stand, glibly claiming it was a coincidence that the heart attack occurred after the EKG's he had taken and the various follow-up appointments. It wasn't cold in the courtroom, but I shivered and pulled my jacket tighter, then glared at him, unable to believe he could say that with a straight face. The words of Rob's surgeon three years before drummed in my head. *This didn't happen overnight and should have been diagnosed way before it ever got this far.* I settled back in my seat. Surely the jury would see the negligence that had occurred, almost costing my husband his life.

Chapter 26

CHERYL

CHILLED TO THE BONE—WHY ROB WAS FROZEN

IT WAS LATE THAT NIGHT BY THE TIME everyone had gone home. Our whole family took over a conference room across from Rob's room. The young doctor in charge of watching over him came into the conference room and gave us all a final update on his condition.

At that point they planned to try a new freezing procedure in the morning that would freeze his body for twenty-four hours and then defrost him for the next twelve hours. With this procedure the body temperature cannot drop below thirty-two degrees, or the patient's heart can go into cardiac arrest and Rob's heart was much too weak for that to happen again.

As I understood it, the reason they wanted to try this was to give Rob's other organs, especially the brain, a rest from working so hard. Anyway, with the whole family squished into this small conference room, the doctor came in and said, "His body went through such a traumatic experience, I can't predict an outcome at this time, but we are doing everything and anything to keep him alive."

By now I was so exhausted and mentally drained that I just

needed to rest my head in my arms on the table. It felt like that day had been a hundred hours long. I just wanted to go back to Rob's room, climb into his hospital bed with him, and think about what it felt like to have his strong arms around me. I needed to feel safe again like I had all the times before when I was upset.

Everybody left after the doctor gave us the update. Sam's eyes welled up with tears and I knew our little girl was finally about to cry when she walked out of the room to steal a minute by herself. The doctor followed to check on her, but Sam yelled, "Can I just get a minute alone?" She hadn't really cried all day, so I guessed she was hiding her tears from me trying to be strong.

During the next few days Sam, Casey, and the doctor became very close and looked forward to seeing each other. Even when the doctor wasn't on shift she called the floor to check on Rob.

I wasn't going to leave the hospital without him and I didn't want our daughters to stay all night, either. They had never been alone in the house, so I asked their boyfriends to stay with them and assured them I would call if anything changed. They needed to get some rest.

All night long I sat at Rob's bedside looking at him, talking to him, and holding his hand. My big meltdown began when the reality of what a close call it was, and still could be, kicked in.

I could have been by myself for the rest of my life. Rob wouldn't have been with me to take Casey to her first day of college. Who was going to open the pool, take the Christmas stuff down from the attic for holidays? All of the things that Rob and I had argued about seemed so stupid now.

At that moment I would have done anything if he could just ask me to make him a sandwich.

It's funny, I thought I would like the quiet time for just me and Rob that night, but I realized I really was alone and scared, like the child I was when I had no one to go to or trust.

If Rob were to die, everyone would go back to their families

INCEST, MURDER AND A MIRACLE

and continue their life, and I'd be on my own. It happened when my mom died. After a while people stop coming around. I don't know whether they got too busy or thought time heals all wounds, or maybe they felt we didn't need them anymore. It always happens and I wasn't ready to spend the rest of my life by myself.

As an adult, I always thought of myself as a strong, tough person and if I could handle all the crap I went through as a kid, I could handle anything. But I guess it doesn't work like that. Some days you can only be so strong.

◆ ◆ ◆

That morning, while the doctors gathered around Rob, I tried to understand all the medical terms, Jimmy walked in. He had just arrived from Tennessee and came directly to the hospital. For as long as I can remember, Jimmy and Rob have addressed each other with curse words when they say hi or goodbye. Maybe it's their way of showing manly affection, but that's how it is.

Jimmy called out, "Hey Fuck Face, how ya feeling?" Either he was trying to lighten the mood or was just being himself, but you should have seen the shock on the doctors' faces. Honestly, I wasn't sure whether to laugh or cry.

I walked over to my brother, gave him a big hug, and thanked him for coming so fast. Jimmy just stood there, staring at all of the tubes coming out of Rob and listening to the beeping sounds of the machines. He broke down and cried, which was something he rarely did, if ever. When I'd called him, I tried to warn him about what Rob looked like, but I guess you cannot prepare yourself for something like this.

It was another long day, but later that night Rob's body temperature had finally defrosted to what it needed to be. It had taken a lot longer than expected and all I could think was, *Leave it to Rob—he always has to do things the hard way.*

- 157 -

Then one of the residents walked in, read the machine, and told me Rob had no brain activity. We had gotten past so much, and now this, the thing that was my biggest fear. I totally freaked out, tears rolling down my cheeks. Rob's boss, Dr. Vacirca, walked in to see me in the middle of a meltdown. Concern was written all over his face when he said, "What happened?"

Between gulps I answered, "Resident—said—no—b-brain—activity."

He looked at the machine and said in a calming voice, "The resident should have said Rob wasn't having any seizure activity, and that's a good thing. It's okay, he does have brain activity."

Family and friends were in Rob's room that night when Rob's nurse Steve decided he would try to take him off the sedation medicine called Propofol. The slang term it's known by these days is "Jackson Juice", because an overdose ultimately killed Michael Jackson. It comes in little clear bottles, is pure white, and looks a lot like milk.

I was told that as soon as the medication wears off, the patient comes right out of sedation. So we were all around Rob's bedside when Steve let the Propofol almost run out. He said, "Cheryl, call his name. Let him hear your voice."

"Can you hear me?" I said. "Rob?"

He opened his eyes. It was one of the best days of my life! We all yelled and screamed for joy. His heart rate raced up, and that wasn't good for his healing heart, so Steve put him back under sedation.

It broke my heart to see Rob look so scared, but I was pretty sure he recognized my voice. That was the highlight of our day. There was some hope that he could hear and understand his name. There were still many challenges ahead, and I tried my best to convince myself that this was just one more. After all, I'd overcome so much in my forty-three years. But it wasn't that simple. This time it was my husband's life hanging in the balance.

That night our girls went home with Jimmy to get some rest, check on the dog, the house, get the mail and, truthfully, to just get away from the madness. I stayed at Rob's bedside again. I hadn't slept yet, but I guess the worry and the adrenalin kept me wide awake.

We had the same nice night nurse and I expected Steve would be our day nurse, but instead there was a new nurse named Cathy. I could tell she was on the ball although she was a lot stricter to our family about hospital rules and visitors. Still, she was also very kind and friendly to me.

At around six-thirty that morning Rob wasn't getting enough oxygen and they tried to take the intubation tube out of his throat to replace it. For some reason they couldn't get the tube back down his throat.

Panic gripped me once again as all hell broke loose.

Chapter 27

CHERYL

CODE BLUE

MANY MEDICAL STAFF MEMBERS RAN into his room again and began to bag him manually. That involved putting a mask over his face and squeezing a reservoir bag on an anesthesia machine to act as an artificial ventilator and deliver air to his lungs. All the lights were flashing. They called for the Code Blue cart again.

I couldn't believe it! Not again. I couldn't do this again and definitely not by myself. I stood in the hallway outside Rob's room frozen to the spot. Another nurse came to stay with me and it was a relief when I recognized her. She was the daughter of my mother in-law's good friend Max. During the code, Maureen sat next to me outside the room and held my hand. She said, "Don't worry. Everything will be okay. Rob is in good hands." That calmed me down.

She went into his room, then came out and reported new information. Normally I would have been pacing as I do in times of stress, but this was one time I couldn't. My legs felt like rubber and I had no strength left. I just sat without moving and waited for information.

Having Maureen there with me was like having an angel

whenever I needed one and I will always be grateful for her and never forget how caring she was. She came to see me every day she was on duty. Unlike the time of my father's murder and the years that followed, unlike the people who damned and betrayed me, this time I learned there are people in this world who are good and do not expect anything in return for their kindness. That was something I never expected. Sometimes in a crisis you learn things you never would have learned otherwise. It made me question whether that is why bad things happen to us—so we learn valuable lessons.

It was so early in the morning, and once again my family wasn't with me. I didn't know what to do. Did I call everyone again and have them race up here?

I watched the respirations on the machine outside his room. I knew it was not good for Rob to lose any more oxygen, because we were already worried about his brain function. Finally I called Jimmy. "Rob is coding again. Can you come to the hospital right away?" I didn't need to say anything more. I knew he'd be there.

I also called Liz.

Right about then nurse Cathy came out and said, "We need to bring Rob to surgery. We'll have to put a trach in his throat so he can breathe better. Um, you need to sign this form." She handed me the form and I signed blindly.

Then the doctor came out and said, "This is the best chance for his survival."

I couldn't hold the tears any longer and began to cry. Rob wouldn't want his throat cut open, but they couldn't get an intubation tube down and he was losing oxygen every minute that passed. To make matters worse, they were concerned the blood thinners from the heart surgery made the procedure extremely dangerous, but they had no choice.

I followed behind the stretcher as they wheeled him to surgery. They stopped me at the elevator. I stood there helplessly, watching them physically bag him so he could get air. Then a gentle voice said, "You have to go back to his room. We can't let you come any farther, but we'll let you know as soon as the surgery is over."

I looked over at Cathy, tears still inching down my cheeks. "Please don't let him die. Not after everything he's been through."

She shook her head, the elevator doors opened, and I watched them rush him in. The doors closed, I turned around, then slowly walked back to his room. I felt like all the air had been sucked out of my own body and I needed to be bagged too. I couldn't breathe. I just wanted to die.

Could this be happening again? WHY? Haven't we been through enough? Why am I being punished again? Is this for having my father killed? God, am I that bad of a person, that you want torture me and my family over and over? Do I still need to prove I am strong?

The waiting was so scary! Jimmy, our girls, Liz, and Rob's best friend James, waited in silence with me for the surgery to be over, and we all breathed a sigh of relief when the doctor came out and gave us the good news. Rob made it through. Everyone always tells you God only gives you what you can handle. At that moment I felt it was the biggest bullshit story anyone could ever come up with. People who aren't going through anything can say it and believe it. But try being the one going through it.

More and more questions screamed in my head. Was I talking to God? I don't know who I was asking. All I knew was I couldn't take much more.

Four days after coming back to life, still in an induced coma, Rob developed a fever and they couldn't figure out where it was coming from.

His lab results weren't coming back well and his trach—the tube inserted directly into an opening in his throat—became clogged again. He wasn't getting oxygen correctly, which meant there was yet another ordeal to face.

They tried to take him off the Propofol every day so they could see the condition of his brain. To this day it hurts to say it or write it, but in all honesty, every bit of the heroic work they were doing would have been in vain if he had no brain function. By the end of his seventeen day coma, I'd counted ninety-seven bottles of Propofol.

In the past I had sometimes complained about my everyday life. Now, completely exhausted, I just wanted my life back. This waiting and not knowing was worse than the time I spent in jail. At least then, I knew it wasn't forever and could count the days until it ended. This time the jail was my mind, and I didn't have a clue as to how it would end. What would Rob be like if he survived? Would he survive? It was something I had absolutely no control over. The only thing I was thankful for was that because of the abuse I'd suffered when I was a kid, and my time in jail, I'd developed an ability to take a break and view the situation from the outside. Like watching someone else's life.

I was able to sleep in spurts, but it was always a light and troubled sleep. If anyone entered the room, I would jump up immediately. Early one morning I must have really been beyond exhausted, because a nurse entered and I didn't wake up.

When I finally did, I saw she was a new nurse and it was clear she wasn't being gentle with Rob. Naturally, I got upset and fully awake. I shouted, "What the hell are you doing, anyway?"

She was using something in her hand while she tried to pry up Rob's fingernails. I'd never seen any of the others doing that. Maybe she thought I was questioning her skills as a nurse, but she became very nasty. Her tone wasn't compassionate or caring when she said, "You'll have to leave the room while I do my evaluation."

Well, that got my back up and I answered in my strongest voice, "He's my husband and I won't leave. I've never been asked to before."

It just escalated from there, and nothing was being accomplished. Finally, I realized I'd better leave and make some phone calls to people I thought might be able to make sure she was permanently removed from tending to Rob.

She tormented me the entire day and wouldn't allow more than two people at a time in the room. That meant if I was in the room, she would only allow Sam or Casey, not both of them. We needed to support each other and I can't tell you how many times she asked me to leave. I was no stranger to tense days, but this one was an award winner. I'd be damned if anyone was going to cause Rob any more pain than he was already in, and he certainly didn't need anyone pulling his fingernails off while he was in a coma to see if there was a response.

Late that afternoon she apologized. We had a long talk and sort of became friends. Maybe she sensed I wasn't someone to meekly accept what she said or did.

Other than that, the nurses at Stony Brook Hospital were all pretty good. They allowed me to stay with Rob all day and night and also allowed far more than the limit of visitors as long as we were quiet. Rob had his own room throughout his twenty-five day stay at the hospital, and they changed his room a few times as he improved.

On the fifth day Rob still had a high fever, and the doctors were very concerned because they couldn't figure out what was causing it. No matter what medicine they gave him, the fever wouldn't break. Time was running out and they had to stop the infection fast!

Rob was no way near stable and the girls still weren't going to school. They were determined to stay at his bedside every day, but Sam had to take a final in college. Even though she emailed her professor and told him what was transpiring, he insisted she take the final or she would fail the class.

Nobody was in good enough shape to drive her, so now on top of everything else, I was worried about her driving to school. Because we had no idea how long the final would take, leaving Rob wasn't an option.

Time for another decision I didn't want to make. I thought, When Rob wakes up, if he finds out she failed the class because she didn't show up for the final, he will have another heart attack. Finally I said to Sam, "You have to take the final. I know that's what Daddy would have wanted. Do the best you can, then come right back."

I could see her reluctance, but she said okay and left.

After she left I thought, *How could I send this poor kid off by herself?*

Afraid I'd made another mistake, in hindsight I realized my daughter is a lot stronger than I had given her credit for, and she showed what an amazing person she is. She handled herself much better than I ever would have imaged while under the pressure of knowing her dad could die before she returned.

Casey finally showed her true emotions when she realized that just a week earlier we talking about how exciting it would be at the high school senior softball game, and now it was going to be played without Rob there. Senior day was the last home game of her high school softball career, and her varsity coach tried to postpone it until we knew what was going on with Rob, but he couldn't.

At the ceremony the parents were called out to the infield to honor their player with flowers and give them a hug. It was a milestone for Casey, and for the first time Rob wouldn't be there. She was so torn between not leaving the hospital for those few hours or letting her team down by not showing up. She knew her teammates counted on her because she was the only pitcher on the team. The girls had worked so hard getting ready with banners and balloons honoring Casey's team number. She began to cry so hard, she lost her breath.

Just as I'd had to tell Sam, I said, "Casey, Daddy would want you to be at this game. You have played for your high school team for four years and he would not want you to miss your last home game." We called her coach and he promised to have someone tape the game so when Rob woke up he could watch it.

Until then I hadn't left the hospital, but when I told her if she decided to go I would go to watch some of the game, she agreed. I drove away from the hospital with such mixed emotions. I knew I needed to be there for Casey because she deserved to have at least one of her parents there, but it was so hard to go without Rob.

People who didn't know what happened asked for him, knowing he never missed a game. Those who knew of the situation came up to us and said how sorry they were. I was grateful when the coaches decided to break tradition that year and not have the parents come on the field.

Casey went to the pitcher's mound to begin to pitch. She wiped a tear as it inched down her face, then wrote DAD in the dirt behind the mound and took a deep breath. Although I saw her look to the spot where Rob always stood a few times, she did a great job handling her emotions.

Even though Rob wasn't able to be there, Casey had a big crowd. When the team was winning, I decided to go back to the hospital, having been gone for a little over an hour.

I thought, *This is how it might be—doing things by myself if Rob doesn't get better.*

Both my girls had really surprised me and I was very proud. They were unbelievable. I couldn't wait for Rob to wake up so I could tell him how lucky we are—that we really must have done something right to be able to raise these two great kids. Throughout my forty-three years I never felt I was good at anything or had accomplished anything worthy. Seeing what great adults my kids turned into was the first time I realized maybe I had done something right!

Chapter 28

CHERYL

THE VIGIL, NIGHTMARES, AND MEMORIES

MY SISTER RUSHED TO NEW YORK FROM California to be by our side. Rob had always been the one man who was consistent in her life and she trusted him, knowing he would always be there for her. She left her two young boys with a friend and took time off from her job.

JoAnn stayed at the hospital with me at night while Jimmy took our girls home to check on the house and animals. It meant a lot to me for her to be there. It was so different than when she was younger, during the years we were torn apart while she lived with my father's sister and had been so brainwashed into believing lies that she constantly blamed me for our father's death. We definitely had our ups and downs through the years, but now when I needed her, she was there. I thought back to the time when I was a child myself and had promised our mother that I would always protect and watch out for her. Now JoAnn was doing the same for me and my family.

She slept next to me in Rob's room on two chairs pushed together. I'm sure it wasn't comfortable, but she never complained. I had gotten my baby sister back and she proved she loved and trusted me again. After so much hurt during all of the years she was mad at me, I was glad and grateful now she was there at my side.

I had always been kind of close with Rob's sister and her support was a Godsend. Liz was my maid of honor at our wedding. We had gone through a lot together when her parents were sick and when she was diagnosed with MS. But nothing compared to what we faced as Rob remained in the induced coma. Not knowing if he would live or die, and whether he would be brain-damaged if he lived, was the worst kind of agony.

Liz remained so strong for me, giving me someone else to lean on as I tried to do the same for her. It had to be unbelievably rough for her to see her brother deathly ill day in and day out. Meanwhile, I was being told a lot of things I didn't really understand. Being an RN, she was able to not only understand, but explain everything to me in simple language. Her love and support meant the world to me.

It was wonderful to know what family love meant when everything bad was happening around me. Liz's daughter, our niece Kristina, continuously drove my mother-in-law back and forth to the hospital along with Kay, Liz's mother in-law who had flown up from Florida to help. They also assisted with everyone's errands so we didn't have to leave the hospital. On the days I felt I couldn't bear one more piece of bad news, Rob's family was there for me.

His Aunt Fran brought in home-cooked meals. If you have ever experienced hospital food, imagine eating it for twenty-five days straight. You would know words cannot express how much her thoughtfulness of bringing home-cooked meals meant. Rob's Aunt Carla always came to the hospital with things to cheer us up. She made sure our girls had gas and parking money and anything else they needed so I could concentrate on Rob.

Their support perked me up and gave me the positive reinforcement I needed so badly. I'd often heard it said that there is always something good that comes out of something bad. For me it was the knowledge of the love and support of our family and friends.

The routine we'd fallen into changed when Jimmy had to go home after being with us a week. During the time he was there, he had been an awesome help to me and the girls. He kept the house under control by mowing the lawn, food shopping, taking care of our animals, and was there for me and the girls every day. I was sad to see him go, however we understood that he needed to get back to his job. He never got to see Rob awake, but after he was home he called every couple of hours every day to check on Rob and all of us.

After Jimmy left, I asked JoAnn to stay with the girls at night. They were afraid to be by themselves and honestly, I wanted quiet time at night to be alone with Rob. Sometimes I had the need to tell him things and then just cry by myself. They say people in comas hear things, but I have no idea if he did or not. Between so many visits by friends and family, I felt like I needed for it to be just me and Rob. I needed to feel our togetherness.

For seventeen days straight I stayed by his bedside. Maybe all the time I'd spent in a jail cell had conditioned me for this vigil. The nurses brought me a recliner chair by the fifth day, saying, "You need a comfortable place to rest."

But, if I reclined the chair, I couldn't get close enough to the bed, and I desperately needed to be as close as possible. It was hard for them to understand that I didn't require much sleep because my need to watch over Rob was greater. I found it kind of funny when they nicknamed me the "Pit Bull." The truth of the matter is I've never been able to sleep much because of my childhood nightmares that have never stopped haunting me.

My most frequent one is about the day my father was shot and killed in our driveway. In the nightmare, I wake up to go to

INCEST, MURDER AND A MIRACLE

school and when I let our dog out, my father lays face down on the concrete driveway, covered in blood. I run outside to see if he's okay. I stand over his bloody body and say softly, "Dad? Daddy?"

When he doesn't answer, I try to jump over his body to get help, but while I'm in the air, his arm comes up quickly and he grabs my ankle. I look at his face. He looks very angry at me, but his mouth forms what could only be recognized as his sarcastic smirk. The same smirk I remembered he gave me when I found my sister sleeping in his bed. Then I wake up.

This nightmare seems to last a lot longer than it takes me to talk about it. Maybe I have always had so much trouble falling asleep because I know that nightmare lurks in my subconscious, waiting to play yet one more time as soon as I'm asleep. New images have been added to the collection now. Sometimes it will be Rob's face while he was having the heart attack, or any number of scary moments throughout that ordeal.

I guess most people have nightmares about monsters and scary people hurting them, but for me the monster and scary person are the same and always will be—my father. As much as I want to forget about that time in my life, my brain will not let me. So, I've never had peace at night. During the day I can push feelings down. When I'm awake, I manage to put up a strong front, as though nothing can hurt me, but at night the monsters creep into my dreams.

It's not all bad, though—my choice is to stay awake as much as possible. In fact, lying awake is helpful sometimes, like when you're in a hospital or when you're waiting for your teenagers to get home safe late at night.

When night came, as I sat next to Rob's bed holding his hand, my thoughts would turn to how he protected me through so much in my life. He had hated my father for hurting me. Watching Rob go through this helplessness now was very hard, but I gathered the strength to do it. The other time I had to do this was when I had to tell Rob how my father had raped me for five years.

During those seventeen nights when I sat beside my husband's bed in the quiet of a dark room, I had plenty of time to remember. Maybe it was a good thing. Maybe that was when I actually decided I had to write this book to help others, and I began to keep a journal.

Rob had told me that by spending time at my house he had figured it out, but he was still crushed when I finally confirmed his suspicions.

He decided to protect me from that day forward and he has stuck to his promise all of our years together. We have been through so much—murder, hearing, jail, all the newspapers, not being able to go out in public, not being able to see each other, burying both my mother and father.

He was there for me after I had a miscarriage, a pregnancy I'd thought was my father's baby. I was only sixteen, and had cursed the life growing inside me every day. I tried to hurt it by punching myself in the stomach, while I sat on the toilet and pushed hard in an attempt to force it out of my body. When I finally miscarried and found out it was not my father's baby, but mine and Rob's, I'd wanted to die. Considering all of that, I can still say that the day I told Rob he was right and my father had been raping me for five years was the first time I ever said it out loud. That will be etched in my memory forever as the hardest thing I've ever been through.

During the time leading up to my hearing, during the hearing, and after, the big question people asked was: why didn't you tell someone before that? I told myself over and over, when you have someone you are supposed to trust, someone who hurts you on every level, who are you going to tell? If you can't trust him, who can you trust? The monster is having incestuous intercourse with you and continually drumming the thought into you that no one will ever believe you.

How many times did he say in a snide tone, "So if you think you ever want to tell anyone, just try it and see what happens." Well, he was certainly right. When it was finally out in the open, and everyone knew the terrible secret I'd guarded for so many years, none of my father's family or his friends believed me. They all feared him and knew what a monster he was, and yet after he was dead he became this wonderful person who would give anyone the shirt off his back. What a joke. Yes, my father would do something for someone if they needed help, but there was always a price to pay.

I think about the wonderful husband Rob is, and how ripped off my mother really was emotionally. Although I have to give credit to my father for providing for our family so well and getting the best care he could get for my mother when she was sick. But, let's face it—in his own way, my father was sick as well. The problem was, nobody knew how sick he really was.

The days passed slowly, and my resolve to protect Rob grew stronger. I wasn't going to let anything happen to him on my watch. Even if I'd finally felt tired enough to sleep, and my eyes began to close, sometimes I actually forced myself to stay awake so I could be alert to any problems. I helped the nurses take care of him and prayed every night. *Please God do not take him away from me, I'm not strong enough without him.*

I do not understand why God allowed me to repay the protection Rob gave me by allowing me to protect Rob, but he did.

Rationally, as a child I couldn't have done more for my mother, but I've always felt like I failed her. That I didn't protect her and I didn't do enough to keep her well. I don't know why, but for some reason I have always felt as though I was responsible for her sickness. Maybe it was the constant guilt and feeling of inadequacy my father instilled in me. As an adult, I know my mother's illness wasn't anybody's fault, but continued to tell myself maybe if I had prayed more or harder or went to church more it would have helped. For years I questioned whether God was punishing me by taking her away so I would be stuck with my father's sick demands forever—so he could do anything to me at any time he wanted to because maybe that's what I deserved.

During my hearing it came out that other members of my family thought my mom might have known what was going on, and that she was just too afraid of my father and too sick to confront him about the abuse.

As I sat there in the hospital room, I said to myself, "I will never believe that, or accept that she knew. She was an awesome mom and I truly believe if she thought he was hurting me in any way she would have killed him herself."

Now I wish I'd had the courage to tell her, but in reality it wasn't all about courage. She was so sick, I didn't want to burden her with anything else. I just wanted her to be happy. Even at the young age of eleven, I never complained about taking care of my two-year-old year sister by feeding, dressing, and bathing her as though she were my own child, as well as doing the other household chores. I rubbed my mother's back and did whatever she asked me to. Anything that would make her happy.

Even now, when I think about that, I feel sick and disgusted because I know I was trying to take care of everyone and meanwhile I was dying inside.

Chapter 29

CHERYL

ROB TAKES A TURN FOR THE WORSE

ROB'S ORGANS WERE SHUTTING DOWN and he needed dialysis to keep his kidneys functioning. I'd been apprised of what was happening at every stage, but when I heard dialysis, that was the straw that broke the camel's back.

I walked into the waiting room, sat on a chair, and finally broke down. I don't think I ever cried as hard as I did that day. All I could think of was that my mom was on dialysis and she died anyway. Now after everything the doctors and I had done to keep Rob alive, the thing I feared most was about to happen. Dialysis. I totally lost it.

Liz walked through the waiting room and saw me sitting there in hysterics. She ran over and said, "What's the matter? Has something happened?"

I managed to choke out, "Dialysis. Oh Liz, they're going to do dialysis on Rob." Then I began to cry again.

She put her arms around me and said, "No, that's okay, Cheryl. It's not a bad thing—it's a good thing. By helping his kidneys he'll get better faster. Don't cry."

I pasted a smile on my face, but just as I'd felt when my

sentence was handed down so many years before, I was at a point where I really didn't know how much more I could handle. Everything in our lives was spinning out of control at warp speed.

The doctors were trying to save organs that were failing because of all the stress his body endured and they still didn't know how his brain would be. I was worried about everything—Rob, my kids, my animals, my house. And I worried about the bills that hadn't been paid.

My boss was calling me and asking me to come back to work, but I couldn't as long as we didn't know what would happen with Rob. On top of everything else, now I was worried about my job.

"Just hire someone else," I said. "I'm sorry, but I have no idea when I'll be back."

I knew if Rob died, I wouldn't be back for a while. If he lived, I had no idea what kind of care he would need and if he would be able to function by himself.

At times like this thoughts sometimes pop into your mind that seem irrational later. For example, Casey's senior prom and high school graduation ceremony were coming up soon. I thought about how devastated Casey would be if Rob wasn't there for her. She had worked so hard and gotten awards and scholarships he didn't even know about yet.

On the third day Rob was in the hospital she wrote an essay with the topic "If there was one thing I could change in my life, what would it be?" It was about how Rob smoked. That tugged at my heart, and I want to share some of it with you now.

My dad is my best friend. I lived my whole life with him by my side and I would not be the person I am today without him!

There is just one thing I wish I could change about my dad.

That he is a smoker

He has been smoking for almost thirty years and every time I see a cigarette in his hand it turns my stomach. I know that every puff he takes from a cigarette is killing him little by little.

We have tried to tell him he is not the only one that it is hurting.

And the essay continued like that.

She won the essay contest and received a scholarship the Mejia family offered in honor of the daughter they lost in the Medford Pharmacy shooting the year before. The girl who was killed was one of Casey's classmates, so that made it a great honor for her to be the student who received the scholarship.

That's what I mean by irrational thoughts—there I was, worried that Rob wouldn't be able to go to the graduation when in reality he was clinging to life by a thread.

Then I worried about my father-in-law. Nobody had been able to bring him to the hospital yet. What if Rob died? Because of his Parkinson's, two men had to help him, and Rob had always been the other guy. My mother-in-law didn't trust anybody else to help, but the clock was ticking.

We understood her concerns, but Rob was not doing well and my father-in-law needed to see him. We finally convinced her to let others help him.

Each day was a monumental struggle. I went to the chapel a couple of times a day. When Rob's room was too crowded, I tried to steal a minute of quiet time so I could pray to my family in Heaven and to God for more miracles.

After they told me Rob would need dialysis, Dr. Vacirca, said, "Cheryl, I have a kidney doctor I want you to use. I'd trust him with my own family, and you should, too. I'll be gone for a few days, but please get in contact with him."

Just when you think things can't possibly get worse, BAM—they do.

Chapter 30

CHERYL

DECISIONS

ROB STARTED THE KIDNEY DIALYSIS, BUT for some reason it was not working. They were racing against time now and needed to get those kidneys functioning. After each treatment, instead of his counts going up, they dropped even lower. The doctors couldn't understand what was going on.

That caused a big issue between the nephrologist and Rob's primary doctor. I knew nothing about the backgrounds or qualifications of either of these doctors. All I knew was when his primary came in every day to check on Rob she never explained what course she was taking, what his counts were, or the plan for him. She talked with her colleagues and then just left as though I didn't exist.

Even though that pissed me off, I never said anything. Fortunately, Doctor Vacirca came in each day and explained all the results, all the tests and labs in terms I could understand. But now he was away and I didn't know what was happening.

I thought Rob would at least be a little better, but after three treatments his kidneys continued to get worse. Then the primary doctor confronted the nephrologist and there was a huge altercation. He got all bent out of shape. I knew it was bad when he said, "How dare you question me? This is my specialty, not yours."

My husband was close to death and because of their big egos, the two doctors stood there yelling at each other. All I could think was, *This can't be happening? What the hell am I going to do?*

As the tension between the two doctors increased, it felt like you could cut the hostility in the air with a knife. Finally his primary doctor said, "I'm leaving!"

The nephrologist turned to me and said, "I want to transfer your husband out of here and get him away from her!"

Okay, this was just getting too bizarre. If there was one thing I learned in jail, it was that when the time comes, you have to stick up for your rights. I'd be damned if I'd let them bully me into a decision. I stood my ground. "He's in no shape to be transferred. You know he's hanging on by a thread. No, you will not transfer him out of this hospital!"

It was a meeting of the wills. He shot back, "Well, if you want me to be his doctor that's what you need to do."

Now picture this: I had tried so hard not to fall apart after seeing my husband die and come back to life, and now the nephrologist and the primary doctor were in a big dispute over Rob's care. Should I listen to the nephrologist? Doctor Vacirca told me he trusted this doctor with his family, but I couldn't get in touch with him and Rob was getting worse.

When his primary doctor came back into the room later, she said, "I'm sorry, but I really can't work with someone I can't ask questions about my patient's care without him losing his temper. You need to fire him and I want you to use the specialist I recommend."

I had no idea what I was supposed to do. I desperately wanted Rob to wake up and tell me if I should still trust a doctor whose treatment wasn't working because I did trust Doctor Vacirca, but that wasn't going to happen. Should I trust the primary doctor who wasn't very friendly to me to begin with and hadn't once really spoken to me regarding Rob's care? I was beside myself. I needed to make a decision fast.

The one thing I knew for certain was that I couldn't let Rob be transferred. That combined with the fact that Rob's condition was getting worse made my decision. I hoped Doctor Vacirca wouldn't be mad at me if I fired the doctor he recommended. Before making a final decision I asked for a meeting with the primary doctor. I had a lot of questions and I needed some answers.

I asked AnnMarie and James to go into the meeting with me because I was scared—afraid I might not remember everything that was said. There was a patient advocate present along with several other doctors.

I began by saying to her, "I'm unhappy that you never address me or tell me what's going on." My voice faltered and I began to cry. I couldn't breathe.

AnnMarie sat next to me and rubbed my back until I stopped gasping, then James took over. They had been there every day and knew Rob's case and my concerns as well as I did. Thank God they were there.

The meeting was about an hour long and by the time it ended I was completely drained. The doctor apologized for not talking to me and assured me she would stop in after her rounds every day and speak to me. I decided I would have to trust her and use the doctor she recommended.

"That's good," she said, "Doctor Wadhwa is the best doctor in Stony Brook Hospital, and we'll get to the bottom of this. He will evaluate Rob tonight and go over everything with you." That made me feel better.

Then she added, "You have to realize, though, there is no way your husband will be able to be at Casey's graduation. After all, it's only a week and a half away. I'm afraid he might have some retardation issues. I don't like the way he swings his arms up and down."

"Swinging his arms isn't really that unusual," AnnMarie said. "You see, Rob sits on their recliner at home with his arms over his head. I think he was simply trying to get comfortable. I don't think his arms are strong enough to stay up over his head on his own."

That night I met with Dr. Wadhwa and felt like I'd been given an angel. I couldn't have made a better decision. He said, "I'm going to do a dialysis treatment overnight and will discuss the results with you in the morning." It was like the weight that had been killing me had finally been lifted. I was a little nervous that Doctor Vacirca would be upset with me, but I knew I made the right choice. I thanked God that night for having James and AnnMarie by my side. I knew they loved Rob almost as much as I do and would not steer me wrong. That night I thanked Birdie and Big Mike for having a great daughter who picked a wonderful husband. They definitely proved they are our best friends. To have family by your side comforting you during the hardest time in your life is priceless.

Things were finally falling into place. After less than twelve hours Rob's results improved more than double. This was almost unbelievable. When they prepared for the treatment, they found the reason the first three treatments did nothing to improve his condition. I was told that the doctor I fired had not inserted the tubes into Rob's neck properly. Doctor Wadhwa inserted new tubes on the other side of Rob's neck and the dialysis treatments began to work. I was told once his kidneys were functioning all his other organs would come back. He received a few more treatments and was on the road to recovery, but they still needed to figure out what was causing his fever.

They decided to do a HIDA Scan. That was one more disaster!

The Propofol that was keeping him in a coma wore off while Rob was in the tube, and he panicked. It was the first time he had awakened on his own and didn't know where he was. The nurse got me and brought me into the room. There was blood everywhere.

I screamed "What the hell happened?" Then I said to Rob, "Honey, are you alright?"

He shook his head, a silent "No!"

Every other time they tried to wake him up when I asked him if he was alright, he always nodded "Yes."

I freaked out and yelled, "You can't take him back to his room like this. You have to clean this up. His children are in there and they don't need to see their father covered in blood!"

He squeezed my hand and I stayed with him. It was the first time I felt he would be okay. He knew who I was and knew I was there to help him and wouldn't leave his side again.

He was coming back to us. The doctor kept her promise and we spoke every day about my husband's results and progress.

Rob improved steadily and was moved up to a different floor where he had the best nurse ever. Her name was Kay and boy did we love her. She was always patient and pleasant and knew how to handle every situation. Whether there was an issue with us wanting visitors to go home so we could just relax and have some down time, or if any of the other nurses did something wrong, she always corrected it. We actually went back to the hospital later and visited Kay so Rob could tell her what a great job she had done. If it wasn't for her he wouldn't have been here. She always pushed him to be stronger and didn't baby him, which really helped. Rob cried twice when he left Kay—the day he was transferred to a different floor yet again, and the day we visited her months later.

We will never forget her and what she did for our family. We all hold a special place in our hearts for that wonderful woman.

Chapter 31

ROB

BACK AMONG THE LIVING

TO THIS DAY, IT'S SO HARD FOR ME TO believe I was actually pronounced dead. D-E-A-D. *My God, who did I piss off?*

As a nurse who worked in an emergency room, I've had to perform CPR on more people than I would like to remember. You can't imagine how many times a day I think of that. Just when everything seems okay, a word or sound triggers an awful image of me being the one getting my chest pounded while my family watched.

Cheryl understands what it's like to have PTSD—she has lived with it most of her life, so now that I have it, too, I feel okay talking about it with her. Sometimes it's in a dream, and sometimes I'm awake. The images are so strong, they occasionally bring me to tears. I know I wasn't able to actually see the medical staff and my family while I was dead, but I know what the fear and anxiety in their eyes must have looked like—it's the same look I have seen in countless other families when faced with the same situation. I have heard Cheryl and the girls tell their stories in such great detail, that I can picture it as though I had actually been aware of everything.

When the doctor told Cheryl he did all he could for me, my beautiful, loving wife—who could have cashed in my insurance policies and done pretty well—refused to accept what he said. She fought for them to keep trying, and I can picture the determined look she must have had when she said, "I can tell he's not dead. You have to keep trying."

Can you believe that? How did she know I would come back?

I try to picture her with our two beautiful daughters standing beside her, all upset at the sight of her husband's cold dead body in front of her. How could she have been positive I was still there?

My sister and I are both registered nurses, so she knows what dead bodies look like. We are around them often. When Liz later told me, "Rob, you *were* dead," I had to believe her.

Many factors came together to save my life. Seven years before, I had gotten Cheryl a job as a unit secretary in the ER of the hospital where I used to work, so she was accustomed to talking to doctors. She wasn't intimidated by them, and was no longer the abused teenager she had been, afraid to challenge someone or speak up. She may have managed to get only ten minutes more for me, but those were such a critical ten minutes.

They put me in a coma for seventeen days or so and froze my body—yeah, I said froze my body. It still kinda freaks me out to think about being frozen like a piece of meat, but I guess at that point I wasn't much more than that. Anyway, I spent seventeen days in a medically induced coma, although I do remember them waking me up a few times and people talking to me.

Then on the eighteenth day, BAM!

While I was in the fuckin' HIDA scan they decided this would be a good time for the "Jackson Juice" to run out and wake me up for good. I was like Rip Van Winkle. I fell asleep in mid-May and woke up in June.

For those of you who don't know what a HIDA scan is, it's what they use to scan your gallbladder. Why in the hell would they wake me up in there? I've never gotten the answer to that question.

So many times I think about how I awakened from this dreamlike state without a clue as to what was going on or where I was. Panic set in. The first thing I saw was a lid over me. *A coffin?* I tried to scream but didn't make a sound. *What's wrong? What's wrong with me? Holy shit, am I dead and laid out here in my coffin?*

I remember moving my arms and feeling something in my neck. Then I heard the beeps from machines hooked up to me. I looked over my left shoulder and saw a face I recognized, but from where? At first I didn't remember where I knew him from. Just that I knew him. He was a respiratory therapist I'd known years before when I worked in a hospital ER room.

"Am I dead?" There was no answer. He looked right at me, but said nothing. I didn't realize the words were only in my head. I hadn't been able to say it out loud.

I couldn't speak. There were tube-like things in my neck and this damn trach hooked up to a vent.

What the hell was going on? *Help, HELP, please somebody, anybody please, HELP ME, get me out of here, please.*

Then I heard something I will never forget—it was like the voice of an angel. It sounded like she was over me, so I looked for her but couldn't see her. *Was she in heaven, talking down to me?*

Her voice had an urgent note in it. "Rob—Rob, are you okay?"

I remember shaking my head "no" and must have had a petrified look on my face. She shouted at someone, "Stop! Stop right now! Get him out of there *now—right now.* I don't care if the test isn't finished. I said right now!"

I couldn't make any sounds, but she said it for me.

What happened next was one of the best feelings I've ever had in my whole life. They took me out of the tube and I saw her. My wife never looked so beautiful to me. I don't care what she says about what she looked like that day, I am telling you she

- 185 -

never looked better. I was proud she was on my team because she stood up to them, fought for me, and made them take me out of that awful tube. Right after that, Cheryl asked me a few "yes or no" questions, and I knew the answers.

Then came the big one. "Do you know what happened to you?"

I thought and thought, but couldn't answer that question. *What happened? Why am I in the hospital as a patient? What is this fucking thing in my neck? I want it out!*

I tried to pull the tube out of my neck because it felt weird and hurt a little bit. Cheryl kept my hands off the tube, which I later found out was a dialysis catheter. I remember she kissed my forehead, and I think she was crying. Not sobbing, but tears rolled down her cheeks as she got close to my face and looked right into my eyes. I will always remember the look on her gorgeous face. She was about to give me the worst news and yet the best news anyone could ever get.

With terrible fear in my heart, I kept trying to speak without success.

"You're here because you had a massive heart attack, Rob." I'm sure that's what she said, word for word.

Many nights I wake up hearing this same conversation over and over again in my mind. "A massive heart attack— me? Nah can't be." Then I remember how I thought, "I fucking told you, son of a bitch. I knew it! I was right and you were wrong." Every time I relive it, I remember how I couldn't hold back the tears, and couldn't make them stop once they started. Me, crying? I rarely cried, and never in front of my girls. Not that crying makes you less of a man, but I was taught girls cry, not boys.

Cheryl had stroked my face while saying, "Don't cry, please don't cry. You are alive, Rob. You're alive and you know who I am, so don't worry about anything. I'll take care of you." And, I trusted her when she said, "Everything will be okay."

They transported me back to my room where I was greeted by my daughters. Yup, crying again or maybe still. *Oh man are my kids pretty! Lucky they look like their mother.*

I was never so happy to see them, and I know they felt the same way. We all cried a lot, and I know now the three most important people in my life held a vigil at my bedside every day for seventeen days as I lay asleep in that hospital being kept alive by machines. Cheryl stayed every night, never leaving me alone. She knew—she just knew—I needed her there and she didn't let me down. Not once. I am a very lucky man. I'd felt such a strong need to take care of her from the day I knew what she was going through all those years ago, and now that the tables were turned she was taking care of me.

Everyone took turns asking me questions and seemed so happy when I knew the answers.

Of course I can squeeze my daughter Sam's hand. And when they asked if I knew who Casey was, I nodded "yes." *Why do they keep asking me these questions? And why are they so happy I know the answers? These are easy questions.*

At that point I didn't get it. I had no idea what they had been told. I only knew that I'd awakened in a very weird place. I wanted to get up and hug everyone, but that wasn't gonna happen.

That day I felt it really didn't matter what I wanted, I didn't matter, and nothing I wanted mattered. It was the worst feeling any person could have. Luckily, I'd been healthy all my life and had never been in the hospital before as a patient. Being a nurse didn't prepare me for being a patient. As a nurse, I always tried to put myself on the other side of whatever I was doing for my patients and how I would want it done if, God forbid, I ever needed the same thing done to me.

Now I wasn't only a patient nobody was listening to, but from what I was about to learn, I was a patient who was unique. Not many doctors, nurses, respiratory therapists or other hospital staff member had experience with someone like me—someone who had been dead as long as I had and come back to life. As far as I could tell, no one thought I was gonna make it, and even if I did make it, they thought I wasn't gonna be "normal." That's when I knew why the girls were excited when I knew the answers to simple questions and was able to follow simple commands. For the rest of my hospital stay I felt like a sideshow freak.

Stony Brook is a teaching hospital, and to this day I still can't believe how many people who weren't even involved in my care came into my room just to observe. They usually didn't talk to me, but would always be talking when they left—almost like they saw a ghost. Yeah, maybe a ghost, but what I like to call a freak. Even today, at times I still kinda feel like a freak and think that it will probably be that way for the rest of my life. I will never be the same again. Is it good? Is it bad? I guess only time will tell.

It was a lot for Cheryl to deal with, but she never faltered. She was there every inch of the way, and I realized how hard that must have been for her after all those years spent in hospitals watching her mother wasting away.

In my room, surrounded by Cheryl, Samantha, Casey, and my mother, I was still trying to understand what was happening to me. I'd been transferred from the CCU (Cardiac Care Unit) on the fifth floor to a room on the seventeenth floor. I'm told my nurses in the CCU were wonderful, but I have no memory of that time.

My memories from the time I awoke in the HIDA scan are very vivid, sometimes more vivid than I would like. I really don't want to relive those moments, but the choice isn't mine. Kay, oh that Kay—my new nurse was the best nurse I have ever met, and believe me I don't think I would have survived without the fantastic care she gave me. I know a lot of nurses and a lot of good nurses, at that. However, for me, there are none better than Kay, except maybe Cheryl. Kay will always be a really good memory from a very bad time.

INCEST, MURDER AND A MIRACLE

Nothing was too much for her to do for me. Even though patients weren't allowed to have more than three or four visitors at a time, sometimes there were over ten people in my room. We couldn't tell people to stay away. Let me correct that. I couldn't tell anybody anything yet with this damn vent hooked up to me, and anyway, it wouldn't have been right to turn them away. Looking and feeling the way I did, I can tell you I really didn't want to see many visitors at that point, but so many people were concerned for me, I am still grateful to them. I knew I must have looked like hell and I am a kinda vain person. For good or for bad, it is me and I can't help that.

I was weak, vulnerable, and pretty pathetic, which wasn't an image I wanted to portray. My beautiful daughters took a few shots of me and sent them to my phone, maybe to remind me of what I looked like. I am kinda glad they did, because it gives me a little more perspective about what I went through. You know how they say a picture is worth a thousand words? I had no idea they were on my phone, so seeing them was sort of surreal. When I asked my girls why they did that, they just laughed and said, "It's our way of showing you why we were so scared."

Again, thank you, God. I have never really been a religious man. I do believe in God and Heaven—however, I am no holy roller. My relationship with God is mine. We raised our girls Catholic and have gone to church sporadically. We went when we needed to go for the girls to complete their religious goals, and maybe a few more times over the years, but not on a consistent basis. Considering everything, now sometimes I wish we would, but life gets in the way. After knowing how close I was to having everything including my life taken away from me, I do thank God for all that I have and was given back. I still don't really know why I was saved, and in a way I'm a little afraid of what I'm supposed to do with my newfound life, so I just went back to doing what I do.

- 189 -

Some people tell me I already do God's work by being a nurse and taking care of cancer patients. Still, I'm not sure if there is a bigger plan for me and wish it was possible for somebody to just let me know. Until then, I will continue to be the best husband, father, and nurse I can be.

Chapter 32

CHERYL

AFTER THE MAIN CRISIS PASSED

WE MADE IT THROUGH THE NEXT FEW weeks without more serious setbacks. Rob was no longer in critical condition, literally hovering between life and death, so the nurses could not allow me to sleep in his room. With the new arrangement I left the hospital late, around eleven-thirty at night, and by the time I walked to my car in the parking lot and drove home it would be midnight.

I checked the mail and did some things around the house, and tried to get to bed by two in the morning. That didn't mean I'd fall asleep right away. I woke up at six, showered, and drove back to the hospital to be there by eight. I was determined to be with Rob as many hours as possible and make sure everything was being done the way it should be. Our roles were definitely reversed during this time. I had become the protector, but it was taking its toll on me.

I tried not to let it bother me when people said, "Cheryl, are you okay? You look terrible." Or, "Cheryl, you can't let yourself go. Rob needs you to be healthy and strong when he gets home." Like I didn't know that.

At least when I had slept at the hospital I was able to get some rest, but now with all of the going back and forth I was falling off my feet. When I was at the hospital, if I wasn't helping the nurses, I sat alongside Rob's bed with my feet hanging down. After a while my ankles began to look like cankles. That's a condition where the ankles are so swollen you can't tell where they end and the calf begins.

I'm a person who has to feel useful and the nurses loved me. I cleaned Rob's trach, gave him baths in bed, and helped change the sheets. I did everything I possibly could. Whenever he tried to stand, he got dizzy and sometimes threw up. The medications gave him loose bowel movements, and I helped to clean him up.

He'd get so embarrassed and upset with himself, but I'd say, "It's not your fault. The nurses don't mind. You know, that's one of the things they are here for. They know it upsets you, but it can't be helped." That was the worst for him and my heart went out to my husband.

We had fallen into a routine and I could tell he was feeling a little better. I washed his body and his hair every day. Then I applied cream on him to keep his body from peeling and rubbed Vaseline on his lips because they were so dry. I tried to shave him but quickly found out I'm no barber, so the nurses took over for me. Every night we exercised his arms and legs to keep the muscles strong. It was a lot of work, but when I saw the progress each day, it made it all worth doing.

One of the problems was that he wasn't allowed to eat or drink anything and he got so thirsty. They just wanted me to feed him ice chips with this sponge on a stick, so I dunked the sponge into a cup of coke and fed it to him. He would smile because he wanted a drink so bad. To make matters worse, he watched TV commercials all day long that made the foods and drinks so tempting.

His frustration finally built to the point that he pulled out the feeding tube. When they said they would have to reinsert it, he refused. Being a nurse he knew the rules, but like many in the medical profession, by that time he was a bad patient. They wound up doing a throat evaluation and discovered he was in good enough shape for them to begin to allow him drinks and soft foods. He couldn't have been happier if he'd won the lottery.

I was downstairs at the cafe and James was with Rob. James called on my cell phone and said, "Rob wants a Coke. Can you bring one when you come back?"

I figured he just wanted me to dip the sponge in it to give him a taste, so I bought a Coke and brought it to his room. To my surprise, when I got there James said, "Hey, good news. He is allowed to drink that Coke now."

They put a voice box cover over his trach and he spoke for the first time in twenty days. That was the best day yet besides the day he was able to stand and hug me as I held him, or the day I was cleaning his trach and he stole a little peck on my cheek. Things like that got me through the harrowing days plus my determination that nothing would happen to him on my watch. My heart soared. I knew lots of work was ahead, but Rob was coming back to us just the way he left us, or so I thought.

In some ways, the last five days in the hospital were the hardest. He felt better and wanted to go home and he wanted to see our dog Rocky. One day I drove his truck to the hospital because it hadn't been started for a while. It's very loud, and you can hear that truck all the way down the street. Anyway, I got home, pulled into the driveway, and when I opened the front door our dog jumped like there was a fire in the house. I walked in and Rocky just looked at me. Then he went to the door and kept looking. When I realized he heard the sound of Rob's truck and thought it would be Rob coming through the door, I felt terrible and so sad for our poor dog.

I told Rob what happened and he started to cry. It is typical for a patient to be extremely emotional after going through something as major as Rob had, so I wasn't surprised that he cried a lot in the hospital. He cried when he saw the video of Casey's last game, when he heard of everything we all had gone through, and especially when he realized how close he had come to never seeing us again. Dr. Mercurio dropped the ball with the diagnosis. He should have detected that Rob was a walking time bomb. Although my husband broke down a lot, he was also very angry.

His body was weak, he didn't feel good, and he just wanted things back to the way they were. Because he slept through the first seventeen days, he didn't realize what his body had endured. He just wanted to go home. When Rob is determined to do something, if at all possible, he does it.

"I want to be at Casey's graduation, I want to be at her prom, and I'm going to do it," he told me.

There was no stopping him. He reached up and began to pull out all of the remaining tubes and threatened to pull out the trach if they didn't remove everything. As a nurse, he knew he wouldn't be able to go home with that still in him. Quite frankly, he was a real big pain in the ass patient, but that's what got him back on his feet. He loved our kids so much, he wanted to be there for them and was determined he would be.

The doctors wanted him to go to rehab, but he insisted he had to go home.

"Look," he said. "The best rehab for me is to be able to go home. I want to see my kids and my dog and walk around my own house. I don't want to waste away in a rehab bed."

He was so determined, they decided to remove the trach, and Rob was able to go home a few days later. I could certainly understand why the doctors wanted to go slow with him. They never had a case where a patient was without a pulse or brain activity for forty-three minutes and not only came back, but came back almost fully functional. Rob still had a lot of obstacles in front of him, so they wanted to make sure everything was done slow and right. But it was clear to see Rob didn't have the patience for that.

Maybe it's a result of everything in my earlier years, but I am someone who suffers very bad migraines. This may seem strange, but the whole twenty-four days Rob was in the hospital I did not have one. Maybe my body knew I needed to be as okay as I could be. Who knows?

The day he was leaving the hospital, I got the worst one ever. It was horrible. We had to call Sam to come to the hospital and drive us home. I was vomiting and had no idea how I could take care of him, but I knew Rob did not want to wait one more day. I was in such bad shape myself, I couldn't help him pack, get dressed, or prepare him to leave. It was a nightmare.

Once again the tables turned. He'd been pronounced dead twenty-four days before, and now he was taking care of me again. How bizarre is that? Someone who could hardly stand without losing his balance now had to worry about me as he had for most of my life. With the worst of it behind us, I guess my head just exploded. I wanted that day to be so special, but instead both of us were wheeled down to Sam's car together in separate wheelchairs. Then we both were carsick and feeling terrible.

Poor Sam was beside herself. For the first time in her life she had to take care of not one parent, but both!

Casey came home from school and helped Sam with Rob while I went to bed. I hated to leave them with that responsibility knowing Rob couldn't even pee by himself, but until I could get rid of this headache I was no use to them.

Rob said, "I wish I'd stayed in the hospital one more day," and that was so hard to hear knowing how badly he wanted to go home.

"Why would you say that?"

The answer was obvious. "With you feeling that sick, I would have gotten more help at the hospital."

Of course it would seem that way to him. It was a big adjustment to have to depend on us, but he had no choice. Rocky was so happy to see Rob he wouldn't leave his side, which made Rob afraid Rocky would trip him, so he didn't use the walker for very long.

Monday came and I had to go back to work, but for the first week I only worked half days. Rob's balance was still off and he couldn't stand for a long period of time to do anything for himself. That meant he couldn't be alone, so I waited until Casey came home from school and then I left for work. My boss was not happy that I was only working part of the time but I tried my best to make things work out. If I learned anything from this whole experience, it's that my family is most important and I will not sacrifice being there for them for anyone or anything.

As we had discovered in the worst way less than a month earlier, you never know what tomorrow brings!

Chapter 33

ROB

THE ROAD TO RECOVERY

AFTER I AWAKENED FROM MY COMA I was a real pain in the ass to the medical staff. All I wanted to do was go home—I wanted out of that place and I wanted all those tubes in my body gone. Not only that, what I really wanted was to be able to drink some soda, so I did what I thought would be right and removed the tube.

When the nurse walked in and saw what I did, I lied and told her it fell out while I was holding it in my hand.

"Well," she said, "then we'll just have to reinsert it."

As a nurse, I knew a patient can refuse any treatment, so I fixed her with a stare and said, "No. You are not going to reinsert it."

The nurse was obviously shaken. "But, that's the way you're getting fed and the way you receive all your medications." My refusal to have it reinserted made the doctor so mad she threatened to put me back into a medical coma.

Still I refused, and won that battle. They had to order a swallow evaluation to make sure everything was going into my stomach and not my lungs. When the swallow evaluation went okay, they didn't forcefully reinsert the tube, and they let me drink and eat. Boy, did I feel good.

I felt the old Rob was on his way back. It also reinforced to me that with all my medical knowledge I had the ability to assert myself to the staff, and believe me, I used that to my advantage.

Looking back, it probably wasn't the right thing to do, but I really didn't care at that point. As the days progressed, I got more and more antsy to get out and go home. Finally, a doctor said I would have to stay in over the weekend if they didn't remove the trach in my neck by Friday. I was determined to go home and not stay the weekend.

When he left and the nurse came in, I told her if the trach wasn't removed I would yank it out myself.

"Please," she said, "don't do that. I'll have it taken out as quickly as I can."

I promised her if she would do that I would leave it alone. Both of us kept our promises.

They removed it and called a physical therapy consult. The physical therapist knew Cheryl and spent most of the time in my room talking to her. He told her how good it was to see her. I remember thinking, "Hey Fuck Face, I'm right here and I'm not dead." I know I looked pathetic, but at that point didn't feel that way.

He said, "I can't clear you to go home. You'll have to go to a rehab center first."

That wasn't going to happen without a fight. "No fucking way! I'm going home."

He gave a harsh laugh and said, "Okay, let's do it this way. If you can walk around the whole floor twice and go up and down the stairs I'll let you go home."

I know he never thought I would be able to do it. After all I hadn't moved for almost a month. I figured if that was all I had to do, it would be a piece of cake. Little did I realize how hard it was going to be.

For the first attempt I barely got out of my room, let alone down the hall. I felt completely defeated.

The next day, after working the muscles in my legs all night, I was ready for him.

I'll always remember the look on his face when he said, "Wanna try it again? Maybe you should just go to rehab."

We got around the hall once and I was totally exhausted, but knew I couldn't stop. He said, "So, you want to go again, or just stop now?"

I'll never know where I got the strength, but I shook my head and told him to keep going. That second walk is still the longest walk I ever had to take. Halfway around the hall we came to the steps and he told me to walk up and down. They looked like an insurmountable amount of steps when in reality there were only five or six. It took everything in me to get up the steps, but I did and then finished the loop around the hall.

When I got back in bed I said triumphantly, "Well, I did it. Guess you gotta let me go home now."

He gave me a strange look before he said, "Are you sure you want to go home?"

Yeah asshole, I do, I thought, but I said, "Hey, a deal is a deal."

I could see he didn't want to, but he finally agreed.

To the surprise of the medical staff I was discharged a few days later. Then the real test began for my family.

They were getting tired of the thirty minute drive to the hospital and dealing with the parking nightmare. I knew my dog Rocky really wanted to see me and I needed to see him, too.

It had been a month since I'd left my dog and couldn't remember if I said goodbye the night I left. I always kissed him and patted him on the head before I walked out the door. Even though I spent most of the time in the hospital sleeping, I knew my dog was awake and missing me.

At last discharge day came. I felt so bad that Cheryl was

suffering from an awful migraine headache, but I really wanted to go home. I was ready, but she wasn't.

When Samantha arrived, they put Cheryl in a wheelchair, put me in a wheelchair, and wheeled the two of us down the hall to send us on our way. The woman who had been my rock during everything was now being wheeled beside me, almost as much a basket case as I was. Under other circumstances, the scene could have been funny.

During the long ride home I got car sick. I had balance problems, and the motion was too much for me to handle. At last we arrived at the house and I got out of Sam's car with my walker. Our neighbor was outside and came over to greet me and helped me inside.

Rocky was so happy to see me and I was delighted to see him. Dogs have this sixth sense, and he must have known I wasn't right because he didn't jump up on me like he usually did. He was an Akita/Shepherd mix and weighed about 150 pounds. Had Rocky jumped on me, he would have knocked me over. Somehow he knew that and was very gentle.

I was really happy to be home, but Cheryl was so sick by then she couldn't help me at all most of that day. I still thank God Samantha was there or I might have had to go back to that damn hospital.

The first few days home were terrible for my family. I really couldn't do anything for myself without assistance. Even trying to urinate was an adventure because I had no balance and had to hold onto my walker when I stood up. I wasn't able to pull my pants down or even hold the urinal, let alone try to make it to the bathroom. My wife and daughters had to see more than they should have, but never complained. I was the only one complaining.

Against all odds, I attended Casey's graduation. I might have looked pathetic with my wheelchair and walker, but was as proud as any father could be. It was a very special day and I was determined to be there. I had missed all the achievement ceremonies, so the school made a point of announcing them again. And I was also able to see Casey and her boyfriend, Jon, all dressed up for their prom.

Casey's boyfriend, who had been like part of our family for more than five years, was like a bright spot on a dark day. The whole time I was in the hospital, and even after I was released and back home, he remained as close to us as a son. Jon took over chores I couldn't do and was ready to do anything he could to help.

I had to go to outpatient physical therapy and didn't have the fifty dollar copayment each time. My boss, Doctor Vacirca, paid for all my visits. He said, "Anything to get you back here. We need you."

The first time I walked in for my therapy, the therapist looked at me with my walker and dressing on my neck where my trach had been placed and said, "What am I supposed to do for you?"

Feeling like a freak again, or maybe still, I shrugged at him and said with a nasty sneer, "Well, you're the therapist. Shouldn't you know?"

"Yeah, I should, but I've never encountered anyone like you before—someone who had been dead for almost an hour and is now in my care."

I said, "Let's start with my balance. My left side really feels very weak."

He laid out his plan for me and had a very nice young lady help me through it. We did strengthening exercises for almost an hour three times a week. To this day I still get a sick feeling in my stomach when I pass that physical therapy office. I hated it so much, but knew I had to do it.

During the first few months I also had visits with multiple

doctors. I felt like things weren't moving fast enough, but they all told me to wait a year before I got upset. They said by the end of the first year I would get back whatever functions were going to come back. I was so frustrated. I had gone to sleep in May in perfect shape and woke up in June so fucked up. I was miserable and made everyone around me miserable by lashing out at all the wrong people. As I fell into a deep depression, thoughts of suicide entered into my mind.

Chapter 34

ROB

CRYING ON THE INSIDE

MY FAMILY COULDN'T UNDERSTAND why I was so miserable and it was hard for me to explain my feelings.

When one of the doctors said, "Instead of concentrating on what you can't do, maybe you should be grateful for what you can," that only made me more angry. At last I was able to go back to work, but I had to put on a front for my oncology patients and coworkers who were so happy to have me back. They had no clue what I was going through, so I was able to pull the wool over their eyes.

There was no way they could know the degree of depression I was fighting and the feeling that the old Rob had died on May 14, 2012. I'd lost the person I'd been. It really cut when they said things like, "It feels as if you never left. Why, you seem like the same person."

Boy, were they wrong. If I was an actor, I could have won an award for my performance. I put on a happy face so my coworkers and patients wouldn't know how angry and exhausted I really was. I struggled with so many emotions, like not letting anyone suspect how often I considered taking all my blood pressure meds at one time and ending it once and for all. I am not even sure if my family knew I was contemplating that as often as I did. I hated the way I felt. I knew it was hard on my family, but I didn't care. I blamed Cheryl for my being alive.

In my mind, if she hadn't begged for the extra ten minutes I wouldn't be going through this. I remember telling her how selfish she was and that she should have just let me die that day. As if that wasn't enough, I told my wife that she didn't do it for me, she did it for herself and now I was the one who had to deal with this new life and I didn't want to anymore. It all came to head one day the following June. A year had passed and I questioned if this was what my life was going to be like forever. I was fucking miserable. Cheryl and I had gotten into a big fight while sitting in the backyard that day. We yelled at each other and I said some real mean things to her. As I write this, I think that day was my rock bottom.

Cheryl had enough and said something I never thought I would hear her say to me. She said, "F...ck you, Rob, I'm leaving," and went into the house crying.

What did I answer? "Good! Get the fuck out and don't come back. Look at me. You ruined my life and I'm left like this."

I listened to my playlist on my phone and just sat there. The tears welled in my eyes until they trailed down my face. Rocky came over to me and placed his big head on my lap and looked at me like only he could. The song *Not Afraid* by Eminem came on. That song had been the ringtone on my phone for years and has a lot of meaning to me. When the part came on where he says "Fucking black cloud still follows me around and it's time to exorcise those demons—those mother fuckers are doing jumping jacks now," my dog looked up at me with his big brown eyes and to this day I know what he would have said if he was able to talk. He would have said, "You fucking asshole. Don't let her walk out, she is the best thing you've got—don't let her leave."

I ran up the stairs to our bedroom and pleaded with her not to leave me. "Please don't go. I am sorry. I can't go through this life without you. Please don't go." It reminded me of how I had to grovel so many years before after that summer fling I had. Cheryl eventually gave in again, hugged me, and we both just cried. I knew I had alienated my whole family during that first year or so with my pity party for one, and it was time to buck up and change.

They did everything for me and I almost lost it all by acting like I did. Part of it was survivor's guilt and I still have that. It's tough on me when I hear on the news that someone died of a heart attack. I always ask myself, *Why am I still here and they aren't?*

When I watched Rocky die at the animal hospital, it was really hard. We went into the room marked Authorized Personnel, only to see them doing CPR on my Rocky Boy and it broke my heart. Cheryl kept saying, "Come on Rocky Boy, come back to us—come on, just like your daddy did." But he wasn't so lucky. Rocky never returned to me. His love for me is one of the reasons I am still alive today. I know that might sound crazy, but it is true.

After his death I fell into another deep depression and couldn't hide it from anybody. Everyone was concerned about me again, even my coworkers. I couldn't stop crying during the day no matter how hard I tried. I am even crying now as I write this chapter. Cheryl and Casey made me get another dog three days later because they knew I needed a dog. A few weeks before Rocky died we were in the Hamptons with James and AnnMarie because Cheryl wanted to go to the Dash Store owned by the Kardashians. After watching their show, she thought maybe we would get lucky and see them if they happened to be in the store. Well, that didn't happen, so we were just walking around when I spotted a girl holding an animal shelter puppy asking people if they wanted to adopt him. Boy, was he cute. However, I already had a dog and didn't want a puppy, too, so I left him there.

Wouldn't you know it? That Friday the puppy I saw in the Hamptons was on the local news segment called Dog Day Fridays. Cheryl called the Southampton shelter to find out about him. They told her, "We're getting hundreds of calls about him, so if you really want him, you need to come here right now."

Cheryl called me at work and told me to go get him. I said no, but then Casey called and said, "Please Daddy, can we get him?" I told my coworkers what Cheryl and Casey said and they also told me to just leave and get that puppy.

I listened to them, and am so happy to have another best friend in my life. Sometimes I still feel like I'm betraying my Rocky Boy, but Cheryl says Rocky sent my new boy Brody to me to make me happy. She believes in things like that. Brody follows me around all over the house. He is just what the doctor ordered. He even sleeps next to me in our bed. He only weighs about fifty pounds, but he is huge in stature and is all the dog I need. Dogs can be amazing therapists.

Over the next few months I really tried to be on my best be-havior for my family's sanity and mine as well. Then my mother got really sick and we knew she was dying. When Thanksgiving came, we had to put her on hospice. She had been having some mental issues and they got worse after I got sick. I think her heart was broken. First my dad was sick for so long, and then she had to watch her eldest son fight for his life. When I was in the hospital, she was there almost every day and just sat there with Cheryl and the girls, hoping I was going to recover.

Life is funny. I was discharged from the hospital in June and she was admitted to the psychiatric ward in August and never really recovered. In a way I blame Dr. Mercurio, or Dr. Death as I call him, for my mother's demise and I can never forgive him for that. My mother was my biggest supporter and I loved the way she took Cheryl in and never judged her. She was Cheryl's biggest supporter as well, even going on talk shows in the eighties to defend her. Whose mother would do that? Most mothers would have told their son to run from this girl as fast as they could, but not Tina. My mother loved Cheryl like a daughter and took her side in most of our arguments. It was so hard to watch her die little-by-little and then see Cheryl having to watch the woman she loved so much die.

Cheryl was a mess at this point and I knew I had to be strong for her. My mother had been a surrogate mother to her and their relationship was special. They loved each other unconditionally and she would soon be gone. Even when I began to get upset about having to care for my mother, Cheryl said, "Stop it! She is your mother and you only get one, so cut the shit now." Cheryl was right again.

My mother died November 29, 2014, and it was really hard on me. I asked myself *Why in the hell did I come back to life only to watch my dog and my mother die within a few months of each other?* Again I felt myself falling into a depression. Luckily, it didn't last as long this time. I knew whatever other things might happen, I had to stay strong for my father, who was still alive, and for my sister, who was also having a rough time. A few hard decisions had to be made, like where my dad was going to live now that my mother had passed on, and what to do with his house. I feel we came up with good answers.

Maybe that was one of the reasons I returned from the dead—to help my whole family get through this new ordeal and to be there for my dad, who now lives five minutes from our house. Cheryl and I are able go over to his apartment as much as possible to make whatever life he has left as good as it can be. Again I thank God for my family and their strength and ability to bring me back to reality when my thoughts begin to wander into dark places.

Everything was finally going well until that damn malpractice trial. That trial not only fucked me up, but my whole family as well. Looking back at the way we were all able to be there for each other was nothing short of amazing. Some days Cheryl needed me to be strong because having to be in that courthouse brought her demons back. Some days I needed her to be strong because the hearing brought back my nightmares, and other days both of us needed our girls to be strong for us. Then something happened that I still feel is remarkable. We were all depressed and really couldn't see how to get out of it. We wanted to finish writing our book about what has happened to us through the years and got in touch with a local writer/editor, Joanne de Simone. She put us in touch with author Morgan St. James, who agreed to help us write our book. She was the light at the end of a very long dark tunnel for us and for that we are all very grateful.

I know doctors consider my recovery a miracle, more than ever when one considers what my body went through almost four years ago, but it has been anything but easy. I still struggle with my issues every day, but know with the love and support from Cheryl, Samantha, and Casey, I can get through anything.

Chapter 35

CHERYL

LOSING MY WONDERFUL MOTHER-IN-LAW TINA CUCCIO

THIS CHAPTER IS VERY HARD FOR ME to write. I have dreaded it since I began writing this book because it is one thing I try not to think about. When I do, I always cry.

It's a rainy day today and I'm already sad just thinking about how to begin. All I have left are the memories. As we were going through my mother-in-law's death, I didn't take notes the way I have for so many other things that have happened in my life.

There—I wrote it—she died, but as I did the tears began to fall. Writing those words made it real.

When she left us, a big chunk of my heart went with her. Having her in my life helped make me the person I am today. I first met Tina Cuccio when I was fifteen and was totally intrigued by her. She was a beautiful woman, tall and thin with jet black shoulder-length hair and such a friendly personality. To me she always looked like she was dressed to go someplace special, and I both looked up to and admired her.

My mom dressed in a very plain way and never wore makeup unless she was going someplace very fancy. So when I looked at Rob's mom, I was fascinated by her and wanted to be just like her.

- 209 -

Besides being so attractive, she took care of her three children and one foster child like her life depended on it.

After my father's murder she never made me feel unwelcome, but instead made me feel like part of her family. Having loving parents and grandparents was foreign to me, except for when my mother's parents were alive, so it took a while to get used to this new feeling. The day before my sentencing, Rob's grandfather Carl told me, "I'm proud of you. Stay strong and focus on the time when you will be released and you'll be okay."

My mother-in-law said, "I'll always be there for you, Cheryl, even if your relationship with Rob doesn't last." She helped me with all our wedding plans with the same enthusiasm she would have for a daughter. After we were married I tried very hard to call her Mom, but I just couldn't. It made me feel like I was being unfaithful to my own mom, so as the years went by I always made sure she was looking at me when we spoke. That way I wouldn't have to call her by any name.

Then one day, without thinking, I called her Mom. To my surprise, it felt so natural. I am sharing all of this to help you understand why finally having a mother and a family who were concerned about me was something I'd only dreamed about. My own mother was so sick for so many years before she died, I pretty much raised myself from the time I was very young. The greatest gift my in-laws gave me was a normal life. When I was pregnant with Sam, they threw a big, beautiful baby shower and I honestly think they were more excited about the baby than Rob and me. When we called them the night I went into labor, Rob said, "Wait until we get to the hospital. We'll call you then."

My father-in-law had to work, but when we arrived at the hospital, there she was waiting for us. False alarm. We'd come too early and would have to go back later. The hospital was a forty-five minute drive from our house and she wouldn't hear of us driving back home. Instead she insisted upon getting us a hotel room across from the hospital.

While Rob slept comfortably, she stayed up with me the whole night, walking me to the bathroom numerous times and putting cold rags on my head while rubbing my back. After Samantha Cathleen was born, she and my father in-law literally fought over who was going to hold the baby first. They came to visit us almost every day with a surprise for me or the baby, and when Casey Carla was born three years later, the same thing happened.

I had blocked out just about all the memories of my relationship with my own mother because they were interwoven with so many horrible memories of my father. All I knew was that I wanted to be just like Tina Cuccio. She taught me what it was to be a mother, but never took credit away from my mother. She often said, "You are the mother you have become because of what was instilled in you at a very early age. Your mother was responsible for that. I just picked up where she left off."

As the years went by my in-laws never missed anything for our girls and made a fuss over every little thing our girls accomplished. A marriage isn't always smooth sailing, and sometimes we had talks about Rob. She always took my side and sometimes even joked with my father-in-law, saying, "Hey, Bob. Another payment is due so Cheryl will keep Rob." Then she would chuckle and say, "After all, we don't want him back home."

What mother-in-law would take her daughter in-law's side over her own son's? Mine did and I could talk to her about anything. The one thing we did disagree about was my sister. She always took JoAnn's side. If I complained to her about JoAnn, she would say "Oh, she had such a rough life. She's a baby, you need to forgive her."

I'd usually answer, "Yeah, but I had a rough life too, and she always had me to take care of her. I had nobody." A moment would pass before she said in a gentle tone, "But she's your sister, and she needs you."

Years went by and my father-in-law became more and more disabled from Parkinson's disease, making life harder and harder for my in-laws. They needed twenty-four hour care in their house to help my mother in-law take care of him. Her depression grew as she watched my father-in-law deteriorate. There could possibly have been some changes to make their lives easier, but she had a hard time with change and always hoped he would get better. Instead, she got very sick herself.

When Rob had his heart attack, she went downhill fast. That August she was admitted to the hospital, dehydrated because she had stopped eating. She was hallucinating and acting very strange. It was horrible to watch this strong, vibrant, independent woman descend into deep depression.

After spending so much time in the hospital while Rob fought for his life, a hospital was the last place either of us wanted to be, but we went to visit her every day. My PTSD was on the rampage and it was all I could do to make it through each day. Tough memories of my mother constantly in and out of the hospital assaulted me every time, and to make it even harder, it was the same hospital where Birdie died. All of the women I had ever loved and counted on had died in this hospital. Although this was where I was born, every time I passed through the doors I'd lose my breath and feel like I'd been punched in the stomach by Mike Tyson.

She was released that time, but had to return a few more times through the year. Even though she needed so much help and assistance, I didn't mind because I felt like I was getting a second chance. I hadn't been able to help my mom when she was sick because I was so young. Sure, I cleaned and cooked when Mom couldn't, but she was too sick to go out or really do anything. I tried to take my mother-in-law out for a few hours every Saturday, and we had serious talks. I brought her favorite foods and demanded she eat while I was there. I guess it was a form of tough love, but I made sure to give her hugs and tell her special things I knew she wanted to hear. We all needed her in our lives and her grandchildren wanted her at their weddings.

Most of all, I'd say, "I've been given a second chance at having a mom. Your job isn't finished yet. There are so many things you still need to teach me."

We laughed and cried together and I made her promise to take her medication and eat so she could get healthy and live a long life for all of us.

Tears ran down my face as I wrote the next part. Sometime in early in October of 2014 she had to go back into the hospital. This time it was a mental ward and she would never be the same again.

One night when I went to visit she had not been doing well at all, and sat there eating pretend sandwiches with her hands. She didn't remember who Rob was. I asked her if she knew me.

She answered, "Bite my ass!"

I couldn't help laughing. "Why would you say that?"

She smiled and said, "You're Cheryl Cuccio, born May 14, and you were married to my son Robert on October 9th, 1988."

"Okay, okay. I had to ask to make sure you knew who I was."

"Know who you are? Of course, I do. You're my favorite girl."

I fell to my knees and just wept in her lap. She rubbed my head and played with my hair and told me she was going to be okay. For a brief minute she was her old self.

I looked up at her and begged, "Please, Mom. Come back to us. I need you so much."

She flashed a rare smile. "Don't worry. It will be okay. I love you."

I told her I had loved her so much for so long—something I wished I could have said to my mom, but I never felt close enough to her to say it out loud.

- 213 -

She was able to come home for the last time for a couple of weeks before she went back to the hospital for the last time. She had pneumonia and only weighed about eighty pounds. A couple of days before Thanksgiving our family decided it was time to put her on hospice.

The next few days by her bedside were something I can't even explain. We all waited for her to stop suffering and take her last breath. We told her it was okay to go and not to worry about any of us—that she had raised us well and we would all take care of each other and Dad.

Finally I said, "You can be happy now and live your life in Heaven without any pain. Say hi to my mom, and please watch over my family and protect them. With you up there, they will have another special angel on their shoulders."

But when she took her last breath, I had changed my mind. I wanted her back. Maybe it was selfish to know if she was alive she would keep suffering. Rob cried bitterly, knowing it was only a matter of time until she was gone. Now I know the meaning of the saying that you cry like a baby for your mother.

On November 29, 2014, two days after Thanksgiving, Heaven received another angel who was only sixty-eight years old. Why God had to take away another person I trusted, needed, and adored—one who had taught me so many things—I will never know. Not only did this world lose a wonderful human being, our family lost the glue that kept us all together. Rob lost his mother who had given him his strength and courage and our girls lost the grandmother they adored. And for me, that day I lost the mother in-law I called Mom who always treated me like a daughter. She was the best girlfriend I could ever hope for in a lifetime.

Chapter 36

CHERYL

MY MEETING WITH A PSYCHIC

ONE NIGHT BEFORE MY MOTHER-IN-LAW passed away, I was at AnnMarie's house and she invited me to a psychic party. I have always wanted to see the Long Island Medium, but the waiting list is way too long. I thought a lot about whether I should go to this psychic at the party or not. The idea both fascinated me and scared me. I'd thought about talking to someone who claimed they could communicate with the dead for quite some time, but I was afraid of who might contact me.

After my mother died, I asked her so many times in my thoughts to show me a sign that she wasn't mad at me, but she never did. What if I went to this party and contact was actually made with my mother? Would she confirm the fears I'd had as a child, that she would be mad at me after watching my father have sex with me? I'd told her so many times in my prayers that I hated it and didn't know what to do. Maybe she would say she was disappointed in me, although I kept my promises and did everything I could to protect JoAnn.

Worse yet, what if it was my father who came though? I shuddered to think of how angry he would be because I told his secret and was responsible for him being murdered. I'd always been so afraid of him, but now I thought, *So what?* I was an adult, I'd been to Hell and back and I was ready. Let him show his anger and I would match it.

In the end, I decided to go because maybe this psychic would be the real thing and could help me find out who actually saved Rob. If it was my father, it could have been his way of trying to make up for all the awful things he'd done to me. Maybe he was truly sorry.

When the day came, I was shown into the room and we all sat waiting to see what would happen next. The psychic—a woman—immediately told me my mother and Birdie were on either side of me. She said, "They are both smiling and laughing," which made me feel good and happy. That meant they were together as best friends, just as they had been in life.

She said, "Your mother is so happy that you are here with me and we can communicate." As much as I had my doubts, I still felt a sigh of relief. I wanted to believe everything that came next.

"Your mother says she is proud of the mother you have become," the psychic said, "but she worries that you don't take good care of yourself. She says she is always around you and when you see an ugly butterfly she wants you to know that is her."

I was beginning to feel very warm, and a little strange. "An ugly butterfly? Why would she be an ugly one? Why not a beautiful one?" I laughed when she said, "Because then you will know it's her. Wait, wait—your father is interrupting her and her voice is getting louder."

Well, that was definitely a switch. When they were alive something like that never would have happened. My father was always the bully and the boss, but maybe their roles were reversed now. I hoped that was true, for it meant he was still paying his dues for every awful thing he did.

"I feel that your father is holding his heart tightly. Did he die a sudden death?" she asked.

"Yes, he did."

"Was it a heart attack?"

"No, it wasn't," I said and didn't offer more.

After that she said it was something that came as a surprise to him and it happened fast. "He's trying to tell me something, but it isn't quite clear. He keeps clutching his heart. Are you sure it wasn't a heart attack?"

I thought maybe she had him confused with Rob and I said firmly, "No, it wasn't a heart attack."

Then she began to guess at all sorts of things, all wrong. She was the one who was supposed to be in contact and I didn't say a word to help her. After a while, a smile crossed her lips. "Oh, I have it now. He's saying he's sorry. Do you understand why he would say that?"

Did I understand? You bet I understood. My body had begun to shake so badly, I couldn't control it enough to answer her.

"Do you understand?" she repeated, her voice louder now. "He said you will know why he is sorry."

I managed to choke out in a low voice, barely able to be heard, "Yes, I do understand and yes, I know why."

"Well, you need to know this. He said he is so sorry and he loves you and is protecting you. His voice has faded out."

I took in what she said, still not knowing for sure if it was real or not, but chose to believe it, thinking, *so I guess he's in Heaven finally, and maybe, just maybe, he is sorry!* It was something I needed.

It wasn't really clear whether she knew about me before, but she said, "Everyone is born with a guardian angel who is not in any way related to them when they are born. That angel is assigned to watch over you and usually doesn't come through in a session like this."

Well, that sounded strange, but as she explained it, your family doesn't allow them to communicate because they want to be the only ones to communicate with you. She surprised me then by saying, "For some reason yours came through and was upset with you."

"And my angel was upset because..."

"Because you aren't taking care of yourself and she is worried about you. You've become a very angry person and you need to take some time for yourself."

I just laughed and said, "Okay, like that's gonna happen. Thanks for letting me know about her concern." Some general stuff about my mother and father followed, and I figured that might be the end of it, but she wanted to know if I had any other questions.

"Are my mother and father at peace and together?"

She nodded.

Now or never. I'd been cautioned not to give her much detail so that she wouldn't have information to help her come up with answers. Without hesitation I asked, "Who saved my husband?"

She took a minute and told me that my husband almost died and came back to me after a heart attack. I didn't say anything. Then she said that my mother was there when I was praying to her, but it wasn't my mother who saved Rob. It was a male. "Does your husband's father have a brother who was young when he passed?"

Okay. This was getting weird, but I told her that he did.

The next thing she said was something she couldn't have known. "Your husband's uncle who died from cancer when he was young saved your husband!"

Talk about shocked. I'd had visions of it being his grand-father, maybe his baby brother, but Rob's uncle never entered my mind. When I left AnnMarie's house that night, I was happy and yet somewhat drained. I'd finally gotten some answers and actually felt like what she told me was real. Some people don't believe in physics or mediums, but I do.

I told Rob what the psychic said and he felt if there was truth in it, maybe it was logical. He said, "I am a cancer nurse and my uncle knew what it was like to have that awful disease, so maybe he saved me because I comfort those with cancer."

In some strange way, it made sense. We knew what Rob's wonderful nurses had meant to his recovery, and believe me, my husband is an awesome oncology nurse. Rob even said he would like to go to see if that psychic told him the same thing about his uncle.

I do hope my father is sorry and I hope my mother is finally happy and at peace. We have all been through so much and really needed our mom around, but if she is happy and at peace, we are very thankful for that. We have missed her throughout our lives, especially me, Jimmy, and JoAnn.

Chapter 37

ROB

CONSUMED BY ANGER

I HAD WAITED THREE LONG YEARS FOR July 13, 2015, to arrive and it was finally here. At last Cheryl and I would see justice for what had been done to me and my family. I'd been told the trial could take as long as two to three weeks, so I asked to take vacation time for as long as it would last. The people at my job knew how important it was to me and my family to finally have the chance to confront the man I felt killed me.

It was a long drive to the same damn courthouse where I was given five years' probation almost thirty years before. Across the street is the jail where Cheryl served her time—the same jail depicted in the hit Netflix show *Orange is the New Black*, a show Cheryl could have been the poster child for. Rolls of razor wire topped the barbed wire fence surrounding the imposing four-story structure. There is no mistaking this is not a place you want to be.

Memory after memory raced through my mind as I drove, all of them bad. Memories of going to that jail to see Cheryl every day while she was incarcerated, memories of counting every day until she would be released. How could I think anything good during this drive back to the cold courthouse that held only nightmares for both of us? The anger had already begun deep in my gut. This time we weren't the ones in trouble. We were on the attack. I continued along the road on autopilot.

Cheryl sat next to me looking so professional. I could only imagine the thoughts running through her mind. I kinda grabbed her hand and held it tight and gave her a nod. She gave me a brave smile, but I could feel her anxiety. We parked the car and walked in together as a family—Cheryl, Samantha, Casey, and me—all holding hands. I looked all around and breathed a sigh of relief. There was no media present, no circus, and that pretty much set me at ease. This would be different. Not like it was nearly thirty years ago. Maybe, just maybe, this time we would walk out of a place that held so many bad memories for us with a good one.

Looking back, I wish we had gone against our attorney's request and called the local media to cover this trial. Maybe the outcome would have been different. Reporters don't let up on you when they are hot on the trail of a story. At least Dr. Mercurio would have had to answer some questions for everyone to see how fuckin' irresponsible I thought he was. But I guess that wasn't to be.

Anyway we went through the metal detector and found our attorney. He led us upstairs to the courtroom we would to be in. It struck me funny that I couldn't remember what Dr. Mercurio looked like. Then it happened. I saw that prick and the memories came at me like shotgun blasts. I wanted to run over to him and knock him out.

The first thing that registered was that he was so short. I looked at Cheryl and said, "There he is, that motherfucker."

She fixed him with a stare and he looked at us, then he avoided our gaze by looking down.

I've heard the expression "my blood was boiling," and at that moment I'm sure mine was. *That's right you prick. You should look down. I can't believe how bad you fucked up but I am still standing here. You couldn't kill me.*

I had been warned by our attorney not to speak to him at all—to be the bigger man. *Bigger man,* I thought. *Not hard. He is so fuckin' short.* I couldn't wait to hear him testify and try to justify the treatment he gave me. Surely when all the negligent things he did came out there was no way it could be regarded as being the best medical treatment he could give.

One shot, I thought. *One shot is all it would take to knock him into tomorrow. If he still really feels deep down in his soul he did everything he could for me, he should not be practicing medicine anymore.*

I was sure that regardless of anything he could say in an effort to vindicate himself, when he lays his head down on that pillow at night, he knows what he didn't do. Whatever the six members of the jury wound up deciding, he knew he was wrong and that was why he couldn't look me in the eye.

We thought our attorney kicked ass with his opening argument. We broke for lunch and then it was Dr. Mercurio's turn to go up on the stand and justify his actions. I was surprised that the man didn't lie at all. There were times when he conveniently forgot or said he couldn't remember, so I was waiting for the lies to begin, but he was truthful.

Again, I thought our attorney kicked his ass. His attorney tried to rebut what was said, but the objections and answers only made him look like he had been completely wrong. As I looked at the jury, I thought about what they must be thinking of this asshole. The first day wrapped up and I felt like we won that day. Man, was I wrong.

The drive home didn't seem as long. We were all happy with what we heard and couldn't wait for the rest of the trial. The next morning I woke up early and sat outside with my dog and waited for everyone else to wake up. We got dressed and made the long drive again.

The first of my expert witnesses got on the stand and told everyone how my brain took a hit. He works for Mount Sinai Hospital and was an expert on brain injuries. He had put me through a demanding two day brain test—one that I would never want to do again. However, taking the test was actually good because I really wanted to know what was wrong with me. I knew the results wouldn't be normal because I am not normal anymore. I remember one test in particular where he gave me six blocks that were red or white or red and white split down the middle. Then he handed me a picture and said, "Now make the same picture with the blocks." I was doing great with the six blocks and the pictures, but then he added four more blocks and the pictures got more complicated.

It seemed like I tried forever to make the new pictures with these blocks, but every time I thought I had it, it was wrong. The doctor told to me keep trying until I finally threw the blocks at him and yelled, "If it can be done, then you fucking do it."

His reply to that was, "I think it is time for lunch."

I asked him again in a calm voice, "Please show me how to do it."

"Sorry, if I showed you how to do it and you had to take the test again, the new test would be flawed because you would know how to do it."

To this day I still want to see it done. Anyway, I guess two days of this was enough for him to diagnose me as fucked up, because that is what he said on the stand. Not in so many words, though. He was still amazed, however, at how much I was able to accomplish for someone who died for forty-three minutes.

At the courthouse he even reiterated his thoughts about how astonished he was that I was as normal as I was. He testified that my brain took a hit and because of the anoxia (lack of oxygen), it was never going to get any better than it is now. It was hard for me to hear that again, but I guess it is what it is. After lunch that day it would be Samantha's turn to testify. She was so scared she didn't want to say bad things about me, but I tried to reassure her it was going to be okay and I wouldn't get mad at her for talking bad about me.

We are very close and I know she would do anything for me. She certainly showed that when I couldn't even pee by myself when I got home from the hospital. She and Casey helped me in every way and now, in front of a bunch of strangers, she had to say how different I was. The poor thing couldn't even eat lunch, and she kept saying, "I just want to throw up."

Cheryl and I tried to assure her it would be fine. I said, "No matter what or who you might hurt, it will all be over soon. Just tell the truth."

When we got back from lunch they called Samantha Cuccio to the stand. My heart sank and my eyes welled up with tears just knowing how scared she was.

I thought back to when I was called up to testify against Cheryl and the fear I felt all those years ago. Even though so much time had passed, the funny thing is the feeling doesn't change. Our attorney asked her some questions and when she answered her voice was low and scared. At this point I wasn't watching the jury. I was just looking at her trying to give her some encouragement from afar and she did great, really great. It wasn't easy for me to hear how she perceived me being changed, but again it is what it is.

Then it was time for the defense attorney to have his turn at her. I was probably just as scared for her as she was, but to my surprise he only asked her two questions—just two, and they weren't even that hard. After he was done he said, "Nothing further," and let her off the stand. I was so relieved it was finally over for her.

Chapter 38

ROB

CHERYL AND ROB TESTIFY

IT HADN'T BEEN A LONG CROSS-EXAMINATION and there was still time left in the day. The schedule changed and they called Cheryl to the stand. She wasn't expecting it because she thought her testimony would be on Wednesday.

I watched the color drain out of her face and could feel her anxiety. She stood up, took a deep breath, then kissed me on the cheek and proceeded to the stand.

Our attorney began to question her and I could tell she was getting angry. Not at him but at Dr. Mercurio for making her have to do this. For changing our family forever. She had to relive that fateful day and I know it was very hard on her, but she was a trooper.

She described how she had to save my life when doctors gave up on me. I looked over at the jury and could see the sadness on their faces. Cheryl really knows how to tell a story, as I am sure you can tell as you read this book. She was so great on the stand. I wasn't able to see her testify at her own trial all those years ago because I was a witness, but I had been told about her testimony by people who were there, and I was sure it was just as good as what I was hearing.

I was so proud of my family for standing up for me like they did. Actually, I was more nervous about what the defense attorney was going to try to do to her because he let Samantha off the hook so easily. If he was going to go after my wife, I was ready to jump out of my seat and go after him. My heart pounded when he began to ask her questions, and I was sure Cheryl's heart was pounding, too. But again to my surprise, he didn't attack her as he had my other witnesses. I think he only asked her two or three very easy questions and said nothing further. That day ended and once again we felt like winners. The ride home was so joyous for Cheryl and Sam because they were done and we seemed to be winning.

Well, the next day would be mine to either win it or lose it. The way I saw it, they set the table and got on base. Now it was my turn up to bat to try to win the game by hitting the home run. As I am sure you can imagine I couldn't sleep that night. I tossed and turned all night in anticipation of what kind of questions Mercurio's attorney was gonna ask me the next day.

We all went to court anxious to hear my expert cardiologist tell his side of how Dr. Mercurio screwed up and he didn't disappoint us at all. He was very matter of fact and even did some drawings to describe how my heart was in dire trouble when I went to see Dr. Mercurio two weeks prior to my heart attack. He said if I were his patient he never would have allowed me to leave his office without further testing. When he was crossed-examined, he even beat up the defense attorney. At least that's how it seemed to us.

I remember looking at Cheryl with very sad eyes, knowing this whole situation could have been averted with a little common sense. I was so angry (and still am).

After we broke for lunch I would finally be able to look this man in the eye, medical professional to medical professional, and tell him I know how he changed my life forever. I wanted to see the expression on his face when I confronted him. I didn't eat very much that day—only a few slices of pizza. I was so ready.

We walked into the courthouse and through the metal detector. I was focused. I sat in my seat and waited for my name to be called. I thought back to when I was called to testify against Cheryl and I wasn't as nervous as I was that time, but was still a little nervous. Then came the moment I had been waiting for during three long years. "I call Robert Cuccio to the stand."

Fear, anger, triumph, sadness, tension—every emotion you could imagine ran through my mind and body when I stood up. I kissed Cheryl on the cheek and she kissed me. I grabbed Samantha's and Casey's hands for a little squeeze as I walked by, then proceeded to the witness stand.

Yeah, of course I swore to tell the truth, the whole truth, and nothing but the truth, so help me God. It was cut and dried. Why would I need to lie? I had gone to Dr. Mercurio for help and he basically laughed at me.

My attorney asked me some easy questions like, "Where do you live?" "How old are you?" and stuff like that. Then we got into it.

I didn't realize Dr. Mercurio left the courtroom while I was testifying. He had been there every day for everyone's testimony, but now during my critical testimony, he was gone. My attorney asked me a question and I replied "Because I trusted that man!" as I slammed my hand on the table, then pointed to where Dr. Mercurio had been sitting every day for the past three days, but the seat was empty. He didn't even afford me the opportunity to look him in the eye. I thought, *Maybe he can't take hearing the truth, and that's why he left mid-testimony*. When I pointed to where he should have been, the jury saw he was gone.

Anyway, after my testimony we took a break before my

cross-examination.

Something funny happened before we walked back in. My attorney said, "You didn't say you sometimes have memory loss."

I looked at him and said, "I must have forgotten."

We had a little laugh and then it was show time.

He begged me not to argue with the defense attorney and I told him I would try. Well, that didn't happen. Right from the start the defense attorney attacked me and I attacked back. *Fuck him*, I thought and replied to his questions just as sarcastic and snotty as he was. I looked at my attorney and he shook his head "no" at me, but I couldn't help myself.

Looking back, maybe that is what turned the jury against me. I've always been a sarcastic person and since my heart attack, I guess it is worse because I just don't care what people think of me anymore. You see, after I died and returned, whatever little filter I had before is gone and I say whatever is on my mind. It does get me into trouble sometimes. Sometimes after I say something, I know I probably shouldn't have said it. When someone looks at me because of what I just said, I usually say something like, "Sorry. I died and can't help it."

Anyway we went back and forth for almost three hours and he finally said the words I wanted to hear: "Nothing further." I left the stand and returned to my seat relieved it was over, but still angry that Dr. Mercurio left. I really wanted to punch him in the fucking face (and still do). But it was over. The day ended and our attorney said I did great. I am not sure to this day if he was just blowing smoke or being truthful. He didn't die, so he still has his filter.

We were so happy on the way home. After my testimony our case had been concluded.

That weekend we felt like winners. We knew we put on a great case and felt we got Mercurio every time. Our attorney has been a malpractice specialist for a long time and said the case

INCEST, MURDER AND A MIRACLE

was very strong. The weekend seemed to take forever and we all just wanted it to be over and for Dr. Mercurio to be found liable.

Monday finally came and we left for court in good spirits. The defense was going to put on their case with only one witness—his expert, and what could his expert say? How could this not be the doctor's fault? How was he going to try to spin this?

His expert went to the stand and in our opinion he did a horrible job. When he was cross-examined he clammed up, and I thought *This is who they brought? He sounds like a moron.* It made me happy that he'd been beaten up on the stand. When the defense attorney said, "Our case is closed," it was over except the closing arguments, which would be done the next day.

We left the courthouse and couldn't wait to return. Imagine Cheryl Pierson and Robert Cuccio looking forward to going to court. Wow what a change.

That night seemed to drag on forever. The next morning I was up before dawn. As you can imagine, I couldn't sleep. We dressed for court and arrived early enough to have breakfast. Our attorney was practicing his closing arguments. I'd told him how I would have loved to close this case, but was told no way. You know what? I wish I had been the one to close.

First the defense attorney gave his closing argument and I got a little nervous. He did a real good job—not great, but real good. Next it was our turn. We thought our attorney did an outstanding job in closing. He laid out the case in a nutshell and at one point the jury even laughed at how stupid the doctor was. We broke for lunch.

After lunch the judge gave the jury instructions and they were sent off to deliberate. There were only about four hours left in the day, and while we sat in the hallway we wondered if we would have to come back the next day for the verdict.

I couldn't help wondering What are they thinking? How long will it take for these six people to come back and find him guilty of being a shithead? Twenty minutes later we were called back in and told the jury had reached a verdict.

The jury was led into the courtroom and we had good eye contact with them. The judge asked, "Have you reached a verdict?"

The foreperson of the jury couldn't have been older than Samantha. I guessed she was about twenty-five. I held Cheryl's hand in a vise grip, not like it had been thirty years before when I couldn't hold her hand during the verdict.

We both held our breath when the judge asked, "How do you find? Should Dr. Mercurio have ordered an angiogram for Mr. Cuccio?"

At that point, I was thinking *An angiogram? Shouldn't the question have been, "Should he have done anything else for Mr. Cuccio besides laughing and saying it wasn't his heart?"*

Next came the words I hear over and over again and can't seem to get out of my head.

Not liable.

Not liable? How the fuck can you say he's not liable?

The jury didn't even afford me half as much time as the time I'd been dead with hospital staff pounding on my chest in front of my family in a desperate attempt to restart my heart. *How had they decided it was my fault for not getting a second opinion or going to the hospital the day before when I saw him because I had the extreme chest pain? He told me I was okay. How by the wildest stretch of imagination did those things take him off the hook?* To this day I still can't understand.

After hearing her say "not liable," it felt like all the blood was running out of my head and my chest pounded like a sledge hammer. I opened my mouth to say something but nothing came out.

It was just like when I woke up with the trach in my neck and tried to speak. My lips formed words but nothing came out. I looked at Cheryl and saw she was crying. Here we were again in this same damned courthouse, and my wife was crying. I couldn't take it and walked out. I didn't talk to anyone. I just needed some air and left.

While I was standing outside, Cheryl, our attorney, and the kids walked out. Our attorney said, "The Cuccio's have been through worse and you will get through this."

Fuck him, I thought. *You have no idea.*

"You're right," I forced myself to say in a calm voice. "We have, and we will be okay. We always land on our feet."

We rode home in total silence. No one spoke, no radio, nothing. With that verdict, everyone would think the doctor was right, and we all knew he was wrong. How embarrassing that I lost when I'd been so confident.

Wrong? No, I wasn't fucking wrong. However, the six people who were supposed to be my peers said it wasn't his fault. I feel the jury was not made up of my peers. It should have been filled with people who understood what was being presented, not people who had no clue as to what they saw and heard. People think doctors don't make mistakes. I work with doctors every day and many are my friends, but let me tell you they do make mistakes. They are just like you and me, and none of us are bulletproof.

After the verdict that little prick bought himself a new car and is going through his days as though nothing ever happened. Like he never missed my diagnosis. But, I know Karma is coming for him. Maybe not today or even this year, but I truly believe Vito Mecurio's day is coming and I will smile from ear to ear when it does.

CHAPTER 39

CHERYL

NEVER SAW IT COMING

I'D MANAGED TO MAKE IT THROUGH the first part of the trial. Every time I entered that courtroom I had to fight off an attack of PTSD. My mind played crazy tricks on me as I sat there trying to give my full attention to the testimony. Despite my determination, it was impossible for me force the images of my own trial from my mind. They haunted me the same way they haunt me in my nightmares.

The lengthy *Newsday* article on the front page of their Sunday edition back on March 9, 1986, popped into my mind. It was only one of so many, but that headline screamed, "Homeroom 226, A Lesson in Murder."

Back then and even now, forced incest is a very uncomfortable subject—one the public rarely discusses. So, imagine the public reaction in 1986, a time when even the thought of incest was basically swept under the rug. I was like the warrior coming home on his shield. The symbol of something they didn't want to acknowledge, and maybe that's why so many chose to believe I was making everything up.

I did some research and discovered that actual figures of incest in the form of sexual child abuse have changed. By 1991, some studies of incest rates in the U.S. found that childhood memories of contact sexual molestation ranged from 6 to 45 percent for women and from 3 to 30 percent for men, but according to a 2006 study, incest occurred at a rate of an astonishing 27.9% in two parent families of both black and white women.

◆ ◆ ◆

At last we had four days off—Thursday, Friday, and the weekend. By then both Rob and I were so stressed we needed that break badly, but on the other hand we did feel our case was going well. In my mind I was certain that Dr. Mercurio's expert witness had a hard job doing anything but validating our claim of malpractice. But instead, he testified that in his opinion Rob's heart attack was a mere coincidence and Dr. Mercurio hadn't done anything wrong. This so-called expert witness avoided answering many questions our attorney asked. It seemed no matter what he was asked, his reply was, "I cannot answer that!" I guess if he had answered the questions honestly, he would have hurt their case.

My mind was operating on overdrive. *Really? No coronary artery disease, no indication that additional tests like an angiogram were required, no concern that Rob could barely make it off the treadmill after the stress test?* I was convinced the jury had to see how incompetent this doctor had been. After Rob's heart attack the surgeon who performed the life-saving surgery discovered one of his arteries was 90% blocked and another 100%. Had an angiogram been ordered, it would have shown the blockages and he would have been rushed into surgery right then and there.

What had happened during the past few days of the trial consumed our every waking minute. Neither of us could clear our heads and hoped going to work would help. We were stuck in a never-ending cycle, feeling all the hurt, anger, and fear that had us in its grasp for three years. As details came out during the trial, we were forced to relive every minute of every day of the time when our lives fell apart. We both decided to go to work that Friday in the hope of forcing some degree of normalcy into our lives.

Rob's boss was fine with him taking time off for the trial—he understood the importance. But when I got home that Friday, I realized it hadn't been such a great idea for me to go to work.

"Hey, Cheryl, you look upset," Rob said when I came through the door. "Something happen at work?"

"Yeah," I said, straining to hold back tears. "You know how I told you the trial actually came at a bad time for me to take off, because my supervisor had planned a vacation the same week? Well, with me out of the office she had to put her vacation on hold, and I guess when I showed up today all of her anger came out. She gave me a lot of shit, and told me I wasn't a dedicated and loyal employee. Damn. I've been there six years and outside of vacations, never took off from work unless it was an emergency. But why was I surprised? She couldn't even understand why I took off when you were between life and death."

Concern flooded Rob's face. He gave me a hug and said, "I remember when you played all the voice mail messages she left on your phone while I was still in the hospital. The woman ranted and raved about you not being at work when I could have died at any minute. I don't understand people like that.

◆ ◆ ◆

Tuesday was the last day we would be at the courthouse unless the jury took a long time for a verdict.

I quickly learned the thing about closing arguments is that you are not allowed to object while the lawyer is talking. He can say whatever he wants, however he wants. You have to just sit there and listen even though you want to jump up out of your seat and yell, "That's not true!"

Remember, every time Rob went to Dr. Mercurio with a valid complaint, he told Rob there was nothing wrong with his heart, but now his attorney said things like, "If they were so concerned about how Rob felt they should have taken him to the hospital." Did that mean we weren't supposed to believe what this so-called specialist said?

He talked about smoking and said because Rob didn't quit cold turkey, what could have been and should have been a fatal heart attack was Rob's own fault.

Well, Rob did try to stop a couple of times and was able to cut down to only three cigarettes a day, but quitting cold turkey is very hard when you have smoked for over thirty years. Angry thoughts flooded my mind. *Why didn't Dr. Mercurio prescribe anything to help him stop? Even if he was able to stop completely, it wouldn't have helped. His arteries were blocked. The damage required surgery.*

Many of the statements Dr. Mercurio's attorney made were totally untrue, but I guess that's how the game is played. It hadn't been that much different when I was on trial for my part in my father's murder. Apparently it doesn't matter whether what they say is true or not, as long as it helps win their case.

Next it was our attorney's turn to present his closing argument. It was pretty intense and he spoke to the jurors in a slow, clear manner, explaining all of our points made throughout the trial. If the picture drawn wasn't malpractice, what was?

We walked out of the courtroom and waited outside in the hallway while the jurors went to the jury room to decide Dr. Mercurio's fate. I let out a sigh of relief that it was finally over and now all that was left was to sit and wait. *This time I won't be the victim.*

As for Dr. Mercurio, I thought it quite strange that he left the building as soon as the jury retired to deliberate. Who knows? Maybe he didn't feel it was important enough to hear the verdict. Was he that sure he would win?

About twenty minutes went by and we were told the jury was back. Our girls had just gone to the restroom, thinking they had plenty of time. Rob said, "Honey, I have a sick feeling in my stomach. This can't be good. It was too quick."

Still confident, I answered, "No, I'll bet they felt it was a clear decision. There's no way it can't be good."

Rob and I walked back into the courtroom holding hands and stood until the jurors came in. My palms were damp, my heart slammed against my ribs, and I hoped it wasn't the beginning of a migraine. I felt as nervous as the scared kid I was when I stood in front of the judge to plead guilty to the death of my father. The only thought going through my mind back then was that it could be the last time I would be free for a very long time. The same dizzy, weak feeling engulfed me and I prayed I wouldn't faint as I had then.

The last image of my own trial was one of the court officers sticking smelling salts under my nose before I was rushed to the back of the room and immediately taken to jail. I couldn't even remember if I said goodbye to anyone. I didn't even know what my sentence was.

Now, as we stood there, the judge asked the jurors if they had reached their decision and the foreperson answered, "Yes!"

I took a deep breath, sure she would say "Liable," or whatever they say in a malpractice trial. When I heard, "not liable," my legs threatened to buckle and I was afraid I would go down.

This couldn't be right. It was just like last time—a big blur.

Rob walked out of the courtroom in anger. Our girls came running back from the restroom and just stared in disbelief.

The judge thanked the jurors and wished our family luck. He said to keep on living our lives the best we could. Then Mercurio's

INCEST, MURDER AND A MIRACLE

lawyer and our lawyer thanked each other.

I was in absolute shock. All I could do was stare at the jurors. I wanted to scream, "Are you kidding me? Would you seriously want your loved one to have this doctor treat them after everything you heard? You're okay with how he handled Rob as a patient? You're okay that my husband almost lost his life. Didn't you hear him say he didn't believe Rob's symptoms were real and didn't order tests that would have found the problem before disaster struck?"

I was consumed by rage. I hadn't seen it coming, but we were the victims again. My face was hot, my fists clenched, and the room seemed stuffy, the air suspended in space as it pressed in on me. I'd been worried and scared beyond belief when I was on trial so many years ago, but that was about my own life and for something I *had* done. This was about my family—my loved ones being hurt beyond what anyone could imagine. The feelings were so different. The rage building within me this time threatened to make me explode.

It was the kind of rage I felt when my father made it clear to me that he would have no problem moving on to my sister for his sick perversions if I wasn't around for him to rape.

I couldn't move a muscle. I stood there trapped in time, thinking we actually got screwed again by society. I tried to make sense of why some jurors don't care about making other human beings suffer. We had lost so much and our case was clearly proven.

What had happened? With all of the evidence in our favor and everything that was taken from us, for this doctor to be able to leave the courtroom without a blemish on his record should be called what it was—a crime. We had suffered another injustice in our lives! Just as my father had gotten away with his crime by people thinking he was incapable of molesting his daughter, now Dr. Mercurio was getting away with the jury believing he was a

- 237 -

good doctor. Both of these men were guilty of destroying our lives.

Now what? How will we be able to get past this? At least when I'd been sentenced to spend time in jail I knew I had one hundred and six days to serve and then I could try to salvage my life. I could start over. Back then for the first time in my life I had looked forward to being able to find out who I really was. This time there was no starting over. Our life as we knew it before the heart attack that took Rob's life for forty-three minutes and changed it forever was over.

We would have to struggle for the rest of our lives.

CHAPTER 40

CHERYL AND ROB
LIFE GOES ON

CHERYL

THE NEXT DAY WE GOT UP, WENT TO work, and tried to go adjust to what had happened, but the anger was eating me up. A week after the jury decided Dr. Mercurio was not at fault, I wrote this:

I have really been struggling this week. I can't get over the fact that those people on the jury thought Dr. Mercurio had no fault in what happened. Zero, not even a little. How could this be?

I was worried about Rob being even more angry then he was before, but it seems that I'm the one who is more angry. It's mind blowing that I can't overcome this rage inside me. Maybe because I have watched everything my husband has gone through. After everything else he suffered, in the past year and a half he had to bury his mother and his dog Rocky who both got him through so much.

He endured painful physical therapy after he was released from the hospital which was very hard on him but he struggled to get his body and abilities back to normal. After fighting back from the hell his body endured from the heart attack, something that never should have happened in the first place, we lost the trial to some jackass. He's a horrible doctor who cost Rob his life. I know no one would want to use him if they could hear our story. This doctor took an oath before God to help and protect, but instead decided not listen to his patient, not to order the tests he should have and then had the nerve to blame Rob.

Yes I am angry. I am just so tired of people not listening!

Once again society had dictated how I would live my life. They found this incompetent doctor not guilty of malpractice without truly understanding what we had gone through and were still going through because of the actions of someone else.

I spent a week back at work and tried to get back to normal, but finally decided six stressful years on this job was enough and gave my two weeks notice. I knew in my heart that I would still be working for the next twenty years and I also knew I could not physically take the stress that I put up with during the last six years at that job. I hate change and find it very scary to start over again. It's not like just quitting a job. That's the challenge for most people. In my case, it's wondering if people know about me and my life. It's been a long time since so many people in the country knew everything about me and my history, but even now people do remember.

It was time. I had to find some peace.

❖ ❖ ❖

ROB

MARCH 2016. **IT HAS BEEN ABOUT** eight months since the verdict, and not a day goes by without a thought of the mockery of justice that happened that day in that courtroom.

I think I struggle more than I did before the trial, because now I know it is final and it isn't going to get any easier for me or my family. In the three years before the trial, I always had hoped that Dr. Mercurio would have to pay for his mistakes. Sometimes I feel so depressed, I just want to stay in bed all day and not see anyone.

Not only do I have to be on my "A game" on my job every day, but I have to be friendly and courteous to everyone despite how I feel. It's not my patient's fault they have cancer, and it sure is not their fault that I got completely screwed from a so-called doctor, so-called jury, and so-called verdict.

There were so many things that happened that still leave questions in our minds, like the fact that our original expert witness who had told us for nearly three years what a strong case we had, bailed two weeks before the trial. How could it be that he suddenly felt we didn't have a case at all, and we had to hire another expert witness at the last minute?

I know I have to get up off the canvas at least one more time before the referee gets to ten. I feel like I am on my knees, reaching for the last rope to finally get up, but the referee has already counted eight.

While I'm at work I can "be normal," but the feeling never leaves. Since the heart attack my life has forever changed. I was the strong brave one in my family and now I feel that my girls have to be the strong ones for me. I get up every day and go to work. I do my job and do it well. I am able to keep busy and concentrate on my patients, but then when I get home I am completely exhausted.

Maybe it's because I don't sleep at night or maybe because that's all my body can endure now. I am not sure which one it is— maybe both—but what I am sure about is I will never be or feel the same as I did before I met the man I will always call Dr. Death. I feel so bad for my dad who needs so much help and I know I can't physically or mentally provide that for him anymore.

No matter what kind of day it is, I go to his apartment every day after work and use the lift to get him out of bed. If I didn't go, he wouldn't get out of bed and I know he really looks forward to it. I do enjoy getting to see him every day.

He has done so much for me and my family and I try to do the same for him in return. If he was healthy he would do the same for me. I feel I was sent back from death to help everyone, including my family, my dad, and my patients, so there isn't much time to try to help myself. The nightmares are probably why I can't sleep at night. If it's not about waking up in a HIDA scan or hearing NOT LIABLE, then it's feeling like I am suffocating and can't breathe.

Funny thing is most nights just as I jump out of my bed in total fear, Cheryl is already awake and there to tell me it's going to be okay and it was just a nightmare. What a role reversal. I am so lucky to have her by my side, and I know that is what keeps me going.

◆ ◆ ◆

On July 10, 2016, Heaven received another angel. My father passed away after his long brave battle with Parkinson's.

EPILOGUE

IN THE YEARS THAT HAVE PASSED since Rob's heart attack I have definitely learned a lot about myself— most importantly that I am a stronger person than I thought I was. When pushed to a point where there is no return, I discovered your mind reacts in a much different way than you could ever image.

As a child living with such a filthy secret I was able to block things out and pretend that my life was different. Now as an adult, I can't do that as much. Although when I was pushed into a corner because my sister's life was in danger, I did what I thought I had to do to protect her at the time. As an adult, if somebody or something tries to hurt my husband or my children, I do what I can to protect them in a rational way. I want to take care of any pain they might endure. I don't apologize for that.

Until our lives were turned upside down, I did not realize I could stick up for myself the way I did when I demanded more time from the doctor at Brookhaven Hospital. That new strength showed itself over and over throughout Rob's ordeal as I stood up to everyone to get him the best care.

However, the thing that surprised me the most when I testified against Dr. Mercurio in a room full of strangers was being able to confront a man I have such hatred for. I've carried guilt my entire life, feeling that I hadn't done enough to speak up for myself as a child. That day on the stand I had no problem accusing him of negligent care and even though we lost the case by some crazy turn of fate, I felt good about being able to speak up.

I always dreamed my children would be close enough to me that they would not be afraid to tell me anything—to trust that I will help them with anything at any time. And I can honestly say I think I have accomplished that. Our relationship isn't at all like the way it was with my mother. From the day they were born, I've told my kids at least once a day I love them and will continue to do that until the day I die.

I am determined to get through this life in the best way I know and be as strong as I can be. There has to be a reason why all this has happened to me and my family and maybe that's why we didn't win the lawsuit. Maybe God has bigger and better plans for us and knew if we did win the lawsuit, the right story about everything that has happened since I was a child might never have been told. Maybe losing the lawsuit gave me strength and determination to be able to tell the true story of my life, and possibly help at least one person to have the willpower to get out of bed each day.

I've tried to figure out why my whole life unfolded as it did. I needed a reason to understand why I was a victim and gained the strength to become a survivor, and I think I've found the answer. I believe it was so I can help others by writing about all the experiences I have had, and becoming a speaker and advocate for abuse victims. By knowing how I triumphed, hopefully it will inspire them to have the strength and willpower to stand up for themselves.

Even if I help just one person, it will be worth it. That's why I've devoted time to writing this book and endured the pain of releasing all of the memories I've carried deep down. That is why I want to finally come out of the shadows and do public speaking about my life.

For all those abuse victims out there, you can achieve every goal you set your mind to. You do not have to stay a victim, but can become a survivor and live your life with the strength that has gotten you through your abuse.

It isn't easy by any means, but trust me—you *can* do it.

To this day I have kept my promise to my mother to protect and take care of my sister and my brother if ever needed. I have been able to stand up for myself and my family in times of crisis. I have become the mother that I have always dreamed of.

Now I have finished a book I desperately wanted to write for the last thirty years to make sure people knew the true story of the life of Cheryl Pierson.

And, finally, to all of those people who never believed me, or believed in me—you know who you are. I sincerely hope you do read this book and learn that I *was* telling the truth; that I am a good, loving, strong, honest person. If you were a family member, or a family friend, I feel the fact that you chose not have me or my beautiful family in your life is your loss.

CHERYL AND ROBERT CUCCIO WRITTEN WITH MORGAN ST. JAMES

MORE CLIPPINGS, PHOTOGRAPHS, APPEARANCE SCHEDULES, AND BLOG MAY BE SEEN AT

WWW.INCESTMURDERANDAMIRACLE.COM

ABOUT THE AUTHORS

Cheryl Pierson Cuccio and Rob Cuccio provided Morgan St. James with extensive material for this memoir in both written and verbal form.

They are very articulate and the emotions and thoughts and voices in this book are solely theirs, not speculation or fabrication. The Cuccios met with St. James in person and they had extensive phone conversations and email exchanges. Cheryl and Rob each have a distinctive voice which has been preserved.

Based upon their experiences, the Cuccios currently are pursuing giving talks and keynote speeches for a wide range of events and organizations as well as media appearances.

Their mission is to inspire and educate as many people as possible.

CHERYL CUCCIO

Cheryl A. Cuccio, wife, mother, incest and abuse survivor and aspiring author, has been married to her soul mate Robert Cuccio for twenty-seven years. Unlike her own childhood horror, Cheryl is a mother who dedicates herself to being a role model for their two extremely intelligent, well-educated daughters.

Through parental love, nurturing and guidance, Samantha, the eldest daughter, has earned a degree in forensic psychology and Casey, the youngest, is in medical school.

Cheryl has held various jobs in the public, all of which have allowed her to be involved with her daughters while they were growing up, including class mom, dance team mom, involvement in sports, concerts, plays, etc. She takes great pride in the women they have become. Despite her early years, Cheryl is a strong, confident woman who aspires to be a best-selling author and motivational speaker.

Throughout her life's journey she has experienced many far-from-normal trials and tribulations, and intends to use her lifetime knowledge to help as many people as she can. She finally feels comfortable speaking about being a victim and how she became a survivor through strength and perseverance.

ROBERT CUCCIO

ROBERT C. CUCCIO husband, father and registered nurse specializing in oncology, has been married to Cheryl for twenty-seven years. They have two daughters, ages twenty-one and twenty-four.

He has been a registered nurse for twenty-one years with ONS Oncology Nursing Society certification and worked in various departments of hospitals including the ER (emergency room).

He has practiced his specialty as an oncology nurse for twenty years, and for the past ten years ran the infusion center where patients receive treatments like chemotherapy.

After a massive heart attack, Robert was pronounced dead in 2012, brought back to life, and recently was awarded "Nurse of the Year for New York 2015" by the International Nurses Association.

When working with people with cancer, he strives to inspire them while motivating them to accept their diagnosis and follow their treatment plan with confidence. Robert has been interviewed numerous times by the media, and feels comfortable in that setting. He hopes to help many people by sharing his past experiences.

MORGAN ST. JAMES

MORGAN ST. JAMES is an award-winning author, columnist and speaker, publishes the online magazine *Writers Tricks of the Trade* and is on the board of Writers of Southern Nevada,. St James has written over 600 published articles about the business and craft of writing. This is her fifteenth book.

St. James began her writing career co-authoring the popular *Silver Sisters Mysteries* series with her real life sister Phyllice Bradner. The first book, *A Corpse in the Soup,* was named Best Mystery Audio Book by USA Book News. In addition she has written various stand-alone books either solo or with co-authors. and has earned recognition and awards from Writers Digest and other organizations for multiple short stories.

In 2012 while co-authoring *La Bella Mafia,* Bella Capo's chilling memoir about surviving abuse, she became an advocate for the cause of abuse awareness. She is honored that the Cuccios chose her to help tell their story. St. James frequently appears on authors' panels, radio shows and other media forms as well as presenting writing workshops.

Website: www.morganstjames-author.com

Facebook: www.facebook.com/morgan.stjames,

Twitter: www.twitter.com/morganstjames

OTHER BOOKS
BY MORGAN ST. JAMES

SILVER SISTERS MYSTERIES - Morgan St. James and Phyllice Bradner

A Corpse in the Soup

Terror in a Teapot

Vanishing Act in Vegas

Diamonds in the Dumpster

NOVELS

Confessions of a Cougar

Betrayed

Ripoff (with co-author Caroline Rowe)

Bumping Off Fat Vinny (with co-author Dennis N. Griffin)

NOVELLA

Getting Even

Eight Surefire Signs of a Jewish Mother

NON-FICTION

La Bella Mafia –True Story of Bella Capo

Morgan St. James and Dennis Griffin

Can We Come In and Laugh, Too?

Rosetta Schwartz, edited by Morgan St. James

STORIES IN THESE ANTHOLOGIES

The MAFIA FUNERAL and Other Short Stories

(Anthology by Morgan St. James)

Chicken Soup for the Shopper's Soul

Chicken Soup for the Soul: Celebrating People Who

Make a Difference

WRITERS TRICKS OF THE TRADE

CHERYL AND ROBERT CUCCIO WRITTEN WITH MORGAN ST. JAMES

THANK YOU FOR ALLOWING US TO SHARE this amazing true story with you. Abuse and incest are very difficult things to acknowledge, and often the victims are terrified to come forward because in too many cases no one believes them.

You can help to spread awareness by telling others about this book.

Reviews are very important to us. The authors appreciate it so much when readers take a few minutes to leave honest reviews on sites like Amazon and Goodreads.

Morgan St. James

Printed in Great Britain
by Amazon

62084321R00166